COOK MEMORIAL PUBLIC LIBRARY DISTRICT
Withdrawn
3 1122 00304 2079

W9-CIR-771

DECORATIVE PAPERING

English Decoration in the 18th Century
Interiors

DECORATIVE PAPERING

Richard Wiles

WARD LOCK

For Grizelda

First published 1990 by Ward Lock
Villiers House, 41/47 Strand, London WC2N 5JE

A Cassell imprint

Edited by: Emma Callery
Designed by: Anita Ruddell

Printed and bound in Spain
by Graficas Reunidas SA

British Library Cataloguing in Publication Data
Wiles, Richard, *1954–*
Decorative papering.
1. Residences. Walls. Interior design
I. Title
747.88

ISBN 0–7063–6878–9

frontispiece

The Learned Look: create an instant library of literary tomes with a trompe l'oeil *wallpaper featuring volumes on such diverse topics as ancient history, gardening and architecture.*

p5

Swags of fabric tied with neat rosettes to frame a favourite group of pictures are, in reality, cut-out trompe l'oeil *pieces of printed wallpaper.*

CONTENTS

INTRODUCTION – A PAPER REAPPRAISAL

Wallpaper, perhaps more than any other domestic decorative medium, has been subjected to the vagaries and prejudices of fashion. The pattern books hoarded by wallpaper manufacturers in their bulging archives, and the constant flow of new collections, perfectly reflect how the public's fickle fancies have developed, how styles fall from grace, only to be rediscovered some years later with renewed vigour. Wallpaper, then, is not merely a decorative material but a revealing social document.

A Paper Renaissance

During the 1980s wallpaper was briefly ousted from favour by a resurgence of interest in 'special' paint effects such as sponging, stippling, marbling, rag-rolling and stencilling (techniques which themselves hail from the darker ages of decoration). It had happened before, notably in the late eighteenth century, when it became fashionable to daub Georgian townhouse interiors with distressed, scumbled distemper instead of papering the walls. Wallpaper manufacturers merely shrugged, recorded the trend and, in counter-attack, launched ranges of papers that mimicked these very treatments.

They bided their time until fashions once again changed and, to their relief, the nineteenth century brought about a renewed interest in pattern, and the dark, moody interiors beloved of the Victorians blossomed. Similarly, the dawning of a new decade in the 1990s heralded a renewed interest in the wealth of patterns, textures and colours that only wallpaper could supply. Fashions with wallpaper, as with clothes, are cyclical.

It would be easy to dismiss the idea that wallpaper design is an art form: for it is an art which has been rationalized by man's practical mind into a neat, easily manageable product – the ubiquitous roll. But this is art for the mass market, and you can pay as little or as much as your finances will allow. Like traditional art, there are poor quality, badly executed designs in wallpaper, so, with such a plethora of papers on the market, how do you make a selection? How do you choose a style that will suit your taste, your home and your budget?

Personal Preferences

All decorative styles, choices of colour and favoured patterns of wallpaper are intensely personal, but the fact is that essentially you are sticking the product of someone else's creativity onto the walls of your home. Not everyone has an artistic bent, so we rely on the talents of others.

In the mid-nineteenth century it was customary for middle-class householders to employ the services of an upholsterer, who would undertake all aspects of home decoration and furnishing. Nowadays, although interior designers (the modern equivalent of the upholsterer) are available to guide clients to a choice of decor, pattern books, once produced exclusively for such specialists, are accessible to everyone in decorating outlets countrywide.

The thousands of designs created each year by those artistic men and women with a keen eye for proportion, symmetry and style ensure that you, the consumer, will find just what you want in the pages of the pattern books released with each collection.

One of the plus points of wallpaper is that the same design can be printed in numerous colourways, again offering you more choice. Understanding the fact that many people are unfamiliar with the (sometimes detrimental) effects of colour, texture and pattern, wallpaper manufacturers do the selecting for you, pairing like patterns and colours, mixing-and-matching papers with borders, co-ordinating collections to popular fabrics – helping you to avoid a disaster.

Niches and alcoves with antique ornaments on display, give depth to a flat wall – but these are printed trompe l'oeil *features of cunning authenticity.*

CHAPTER ONE

THE HISTORY OF PAPERS

The urge to decorate our homes has been with us since prehistoric times, when our primitive ancestors deftly sketched on the walls of their cave-dwellings scenes celebrating the thrill or the hunt of triumph in battle. Of wallpapering they would no doubt have heartily approved. However, cave-painting apart, most methods of treating internal walls were well and truly rooted in practical purpose.

Tapestry Hangings

The wealthy medieval householder hung imported tapestries on the cold, damp stone walls of his home, and across the doorways, partly to flaunt his prosperity but largely in a feeble attempt to lessen draughts and cut down on condensation. Emulating his richer contemporaries, the more modestly appointed householder used cheaper woollen or canvas hangings to adorn his walls. These basic hangings, which sought to imitate tapestry, and the fine silks that followed, were the forerunners of today's wallcoverings.

During the sixteenth and seventeenth centuries, the most common decorative medium – where any existed at all – was whitewash hand-mixed with pigments to create reds, blues, greens or ochre yellow. It was used on wainscots and other interior joinery. But, towards the end of this period, it became popular in ordinary dwellings to conceal the interior woodwork, using cloth, paper and even leather. Small pieces of patterned paper – rejects from the growing printing industry – were used by enterprising householders to brighten up the insides of cupboards and chests.

Trade with the Far East had increased during the seventeenth century, so much so that fine textiles such as silk and large pieces of decorated papers were imported from China. In wealthy properties, these were used to clad the plaster walls.

On the home front, advances with printing processes made printed paper wall hangings available, and these eventually replaced the more costly fabrics. The paper was initially made from shredded cloth and, as it was necessary to drain it in flat sieves during manufacture, the size of the pieces was fairly limited.

Neither fabric nor paper hangings were stuck to the surface at this period, but instead were stretched over wooden frames, which in turn were nailed to the walls. Despite the fact that the use of wallpaper was quite rare, paper wall hangings became common enough for a paper tax to be introduced in 1694.

Block-printing Method

Paper and fabric hangings were mainly printed using the hand block method, although some were stencilled by hand. Hand block-printing first evolved during the sixteenth century in the East, where it was used by textile makers in order to repeat certain isolated motifs more rapidly: in due course entire pattern blocks were introduced.

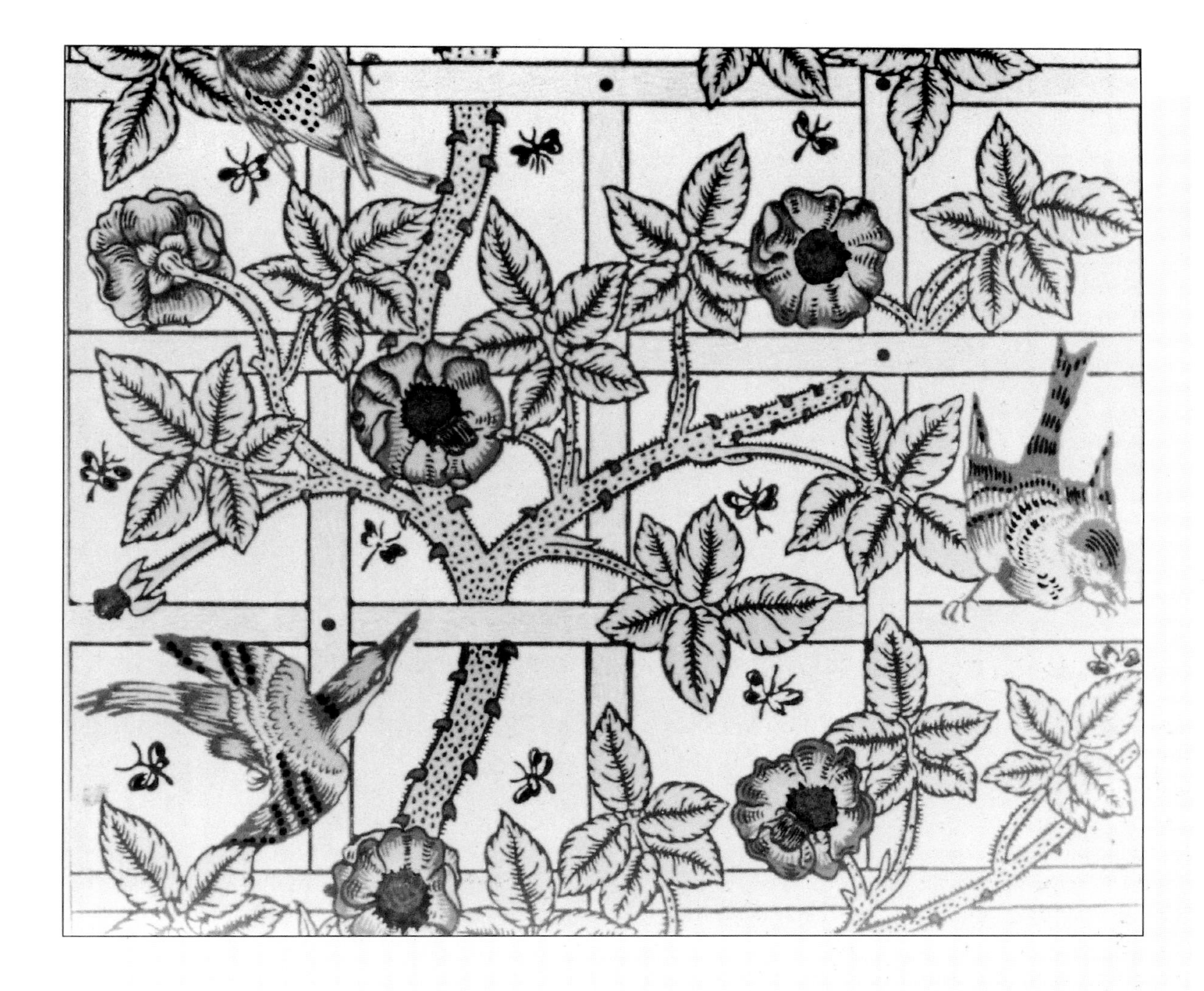

Trellis, William Morris's first block-printed wallpaper design (1864), was based on the rose garden in his home, Red House. The superimposed birds were drawn by Philip Webb.

When printed textiles – known as 'chintz' – began to be imported into Europe during the seventeenth century, print-makers in England and France started to develop hand block-printing as a means of competing with the Eastern imports.

The blocks themselves were cut from seasoned hardwood, commonly pear or sycamore, and the patterns carved into the surface. Smaller blocks, when coated with dye, were simply positioned by hand on the fabric or paper and the coloured pattern transferred by pressure – for instance, tapping with a mallet. Larger blocks were mounted above a printing table; across which the paper was drawn. When the inked block was brought into contact with the paper, so the design was transferred to the surface; the paper was then pulled along the table and the next section printed. Separate blocks were needed for each colour used in the design.

Block-printed designs are usually identifiable by slight inaccuracies in the register of the various colours, leaving overlapping margins or unprinted gaps. Rather than being considered faults, these characteristics reveal much of the appeal of block-prints, a demonstration of artistic eccentricity. Nowadays, hand-printed papers are largely produced using the screen-printing method rather than wood blocks. The screens comprise wooden frames with fine mesh stretched over. Areas of the mesh surrounding the pattern are blanked off; ink is then drawn across the screen using a sponge pad (squeeggee) and forced through the free areas of the screen onto the paper, which is passed along the printing table in sections.

Despite the fact that the advent of modern machine printing rendered the somewhat unwieldy block-printing obsolete, some of the original blocks do still exist in the archives of major wallpaper manufacturers. For instance, Sanderson, who purchased the pear-wood blocks from the William Morris collection (see page 12), when Morris & Co. went into liquidation in 1940, still use this method of printing special ranges of wallpapers alongside ultra-modern continuous paper processes. Customers can select from Morris stock range, or else order other Morris block-printed designs from the comprehensive archive, and have them executed in specific colourways.

Hand block-printing at Sanderson's Perivale factory during the 1950s. The paper was passed along the printing bed and the inked block suspended above was brought into contact to make the impression of the designs.

'Rowan', designed by C.F.A. Voysey, is one of a classically-inspired range of wallcoverings still screen-printed from Sanderson's archives.

Machine Printing

The advent of machine printing enabled continuous rolls of wallpaper to be produced rapidly, and consequently much more cheaply than the hand-blocked types. Machines also meant that printing was more accurate, with adjoining colours and patterns reproduced in register. First introduced in 1839 by Charles Potter of Darwen, Lancashire, the patented design for producing continuous rolls was developed by Potter's foreman engineer, Walmsley Preston, who adapted a calico printing machine for the purpose. By this method, the paper was passed over the surface of a cylindrical drum and received an impression of the pattern from rollers arranged around the base.

Over the next decade, other manufacturers developed printing machines which were capable of printing up to eight colours. Machine printing was originally carried out using the 'intaglio' (etched copper roller) method. Designs were engraved onto copper rollers and the entire surface coated with ink. The surface was then wiped clean, leaving ink in the etched recesses. Where the roller was brought into contact with the paper, the pattern was transferred to the surface. Later, surface-printing methods superceded the intaglio method of printing.

Machines brought wallpaper within the budget of all but the very poor: a roll would cost as little as sixpence. Sales increased from one million rolls in 1834 to five million in 1851, reaching thirty-two million by 1874. Prices fell to just twopence a roll by 1890, assisted by improved machine production and the abolition of the paper tax by Gladstone in 1861. Hand block-printed papers by famous designers such as Arthur Silver, C.F.A. Voysey or Lewis F. Day, however, might cost as much as twenty-five shillings – a price which only the wealthy could afford.

By the 1920s, machines which could print up to twenty colours were in common use. At this time, printed textiles were produced by surface-roller printing, and fabrics began to be seen as part of the overall concept alongside wallpapers, with linked designs and colourways.

Early embossed papers were produced by machines with rollers that moulded the paper passed between them – often several layers at a time – forming a pattern raised in low relief from the overall surface. At first printing and embossing were carried out separately, but machines were soon developed which would enable the printing and embossing rollers to work in unison, ensuring accurate registration of raised area and printed pattern.

As embossing methods developed, machines were used by manufacturers such as Sanderson to print canvas textures and wood grains on paper using the photogravure method (intaglio plates produced using photography). By the early 1950s, even flocks were produced by Sanderson.

'Blackberry', designed by J.H. Dearle, and first produced in 1903, is still available from Sanderson's Morris & Co. collection in three colourways.

CHAPTER TWO

ESTABLISHING MOTIFS

While it is true that wallpaper production methods developed in leaps and bounds during the Industrial Revolution, contributing to the universal popularity of the medium, the way in which the designs themselves have evolved over the centuries is more spurious.

Prior to the advent of paper, carved wood panelling and moulded plasterwork were used to ornament the walls. Patterns were formal, featuring geometric representations of basketwork, combed waves, naive figures or animals. When paper and tapestries arrived, however, their patterns commonly demonstrated a fascination for foreign, exotic countries or illustrated characters from myths and legends. Wallcoverings popular in Elizabethan times often featured heraldic shields, vases, flowers and folds of fabric. Patterns of tiny flowers on bright backgrounds were a typical choice in the sixteenth and seventeenth centuries, while flocked wallcoverings imitating fine silk and velvet brocades was used instead of the real, and expensive, textile hangings of old.

Towards the end of the seventeenth century, influenced by the expanded horizons opened up by foreign travel, wallpapers were resplendent with scenes of tropical birds, landscapes featuring towering snow-capped, cloud-ringed mountains and the intriguing architecture of the Orient.

Late in the eighteenth century it was the trend to imitate plasterwork ornament, and wallpaper itself was largely spurned by the middle classes: the previously popular exuberant patterns and vividly coloured naturalistic motifs were seen to detract from the elegance of fine classical ornament. Rooms were in general plainer, with distempered finishes scumbled with oil paints to simulate marbling, or grained to imitate wood.

Moody Opulence

In the Victorian era, wallpaper designs pandered to a taste for dense, elaborate patterns with complex repeats. Motifs were largely based on traditional chintz patterns, which typically featured tropical birds, filigree arbours, fruit, ivy-leaf trellis and flowering vines, or they showed the influence of French designs with patterns of roses and ribbons. Cheap machine prints were sold in department stores, where it was the job of the housewife to choose the household wallpapers.

Virtually every surface was heavily coloured and patterned or textured, and rooms were typically cluttered with furniture and ornaments in an effort to prove artistic appreciation. These strong, opulent colours and bold patterns – in addition to the vogue for subdued lighting – were partly chosen to conceal the fact that the carpets, wallpapers and draperies were immensely grubby due to constant burning of coal fires.

From the mid-Victorian period, the artist and poet William Morris began to produce exclusively hand block-printed wallpaper designs. At first they were fairly simple, stylized naturalistic patterns, but they evolved into the enduringly popular patterns based on

Monochromatic maelstrom, with a backcloth of neo-classical urns and pictures and striped dado, accessorized with fabrics and upholstery sporting architectural motifs.

medieval tapestries. Patterns showed stylized two-dimensional representations of English garden flowers, often repeated with geometric regularity, and always with a richness of colour.

In hallways, heavily embossed Anaglypta and Lincrusta dados were common, darkly painted and complemented by equally bold machine-printed papers above, topped by a complex frieze.

Plain and Uncluttered

The emergence of the Arts & Crafts Movement, during the 1880s and '90s urged the middle-classes to copy the style of small country house interiors, with plain walls and modest Queen Anne and Georgian furniture. Early in the twentieth century this trend towards simpler schemes, became more widespread, partly as a backlash against the cluttered, over-ornamented and grimy interiors of the previous age, but also linked with a greater awareness of hygiene. However, traditional wallpaper designs remained fashionable for some time.

Then, during the First World War, production of wallpaper virtually ceased, when labour, paper and dyes became unobtainable (borders, however, slipped through the ration net, and were still available). After the war, with materials and labour still in short supply, the middle-classes tended to abandon the use of wallpaper, although cheap, plainer papers and colourful borders were still used by the working classes to decorate their homes.

The working classes had been hanging their own wallpaper since the mid-nineteenth century when cheap machine prints became widely available, and this led to the publication of numerous home-handyman books and journals offering advice on decorating techniques. Hanging paper was not as easy or

Opulence evoked by rich, earthy tones on a complex block-printed pattern of stylised flowers, foliage and birds. This typical William Morris style is featured above the dado and on the ceiling.

convenient as it is today. Most papers had a selvedge which had to be trimmed with scissors before use; and paste had to be mixed from flour and water, a substance which would ruin the face of the wallpaper if smeared.

In response to this increased interest in home decoration, magazines devoted to the subject were launched in the early 1920s. Two of the most popular, *Homes and Gardens* and *Ideal Homes*, are published still, although their emphasis has changed dramatically with fluctuating fashion. At first, however, neither magazine was a friend to wallpaper: the newly developed monochromatic photographs they featured showed the interiors of converted cottages or newly built homes, but both were invariably stark with distempered walls, polished wood floors and Persian rugs. Articles typically dealt with advice on how to strip the loud Victorian paper from the walls.

As the demand for finer hand block-printed wallcoverings diminished, many of the pioneering firms of the nineteenth century sadly went out of business. Some were absorbed into the huge Wall Paper Manufacturer's combine who mainly proffered the cheaper machine prints to the general public.

Inter-war Watershed

The late nineteenth century is widely regarded as the greatest period of British decorative art, with designers of the calibre of William Morris, C.F.A. Voysey and Heywood Sumner virtually household names. But in the 1920s and 1930s few well-known designers lent their talents to the creation of ordinary wallpaper, a medium which had become unfashionable. Nevertheless, although panned by the critics for the so-called poor standards of design, cheap machine prints were still generally preferred to distemper.

In these inter-war years, wallpaper was used in virtually every room of the working-class house: Anaglypta and Lincrusta dados were stuck to the walls of halls, dining rooms and sometimes kitchens for their durability. These tough embossed papers were often painted chocolate brown so they would not show the dirt. The area between the dado and the frieze was frequently covered with 'sanitary papers' which, printed using engraved copper rollers, were invested with a very smooth finish. Coated with varnish after hanging, the paper was washable. Popular patterns were based on damask designs, and all-over leaf and berry designs were also a favourite choice. Sanitary papers were used in bathrooms and kitchens, typically in imitation tile designs.

The Dawn of Modernism

Bright colours – orange, red, blue and yellow – were the order of the day during the 1920s, and were typically adorned with Oriental-inspired patterns. Coal fires created much dust, but the papers were cheap enough to be changed every two or three years, which also kept the householder abreast of current fashions.

The 1930s saw an increased interest in modernist geometric patterns inspired by the German Bauhaus architectural school of the previous decade; this inspiration, typified by cubist motifs, continued to dominate until the 1950s. Colours became more subdued browns, beiges, greens, russet-reds and pale yellows. Pale striped wallpapers were popular for sitting rooms, typically with a complex floral frieze below the slender picture rail. Plain porridge-textured embossed wallpapers were often hung, and the wall surface divided into a number of large panels using narrow printed borders, the corners often decorated with appliquéd cut-outs depicting motifs such as humming birds, butterflies or Spanish galleons in full sail.

Wallpaper production again ceased with the coming of the Second World War, but in the 1950s it blossomed once more with a refreshed vigour. Neo-Regency designs were promoted – featuring small stars and spots, or striped papers in a range of different colourways – to complement the fashion for real Regency furniture.

For those with more exotic tastes,

chinoiserie and rococo patterns were re-introduced by companies such as Cole's, while Sanderson, Shand Kydd and John Line produced designs inspired by early nineteenth-century patterns.

The Contemporary Age

By the middle of the 1950s, a 'contemporary' style of wallpaper had developed, heavily influenced by Scandinavian folk-art. Papers for living rooms were executed in bright, primary colours with blatantly abstract patterns, or stylized flower motifs in geometric medallions. As well as contrasting patterns, colours, too, were set against each other in often violent combinations such as citrus lemon yellow or lime green with purplish tones.

On the crest of a new economic boom, every room in the house could be considered for restyling. For kitchens it was more common to opt for designs based on naturalistic representations of wine bottles, ropes of garlic or bundles of asparagus: influenced, no doubt, by the increased availability of Mediterranean holidays. It was fashionable policy to use two different types of paper in one room, a cheap machine print for three walls, with a more costly hand block-printed or screen-printed paper for dramatic contrast on the fourth wall, centred on the room's main focal point.

There was great interest in the American way of life, revealed in popular films of the day, which tended to concentrate on the lot of the humble American suburbanite. In England, elements of home design and decoration were copied by householders intrigued by a country that appeared advanced and forward-thinking. Open-plan rooms were created by the removal of the wall between sitting room, dining room and kitchen, after the American style of interconnecting rooms.

Encouraging this 'remodelling' of the house, newly published do-it-yourself journals advised on how these structural alterations could be undertaken safely, and are largely responsible for promoting the removal of period ornamentation for 'modernization'.

In the 'Americanised' British home, wallpaper was used to visually define various areas within the through room, such as the dining alcove, or to highlight a focal point such as the chimney breast. Contrasting colours and patterns were used to this end. The *Daily Mail Ideal Home Book* (1951–2), for instance, suggested pairing such diverse colours as maroon and lime-green in a striped and patterned wallpaper from Liberty. Used in the softer green for the sitting area and the moody maroon for the dining corner, the two areas of different function were combined.

Swinging Into the Sixties

The success of the wallpaper industry in the late 1950s and early 1960s – in the U.K., sales were running at 115 million rolls a year – enabled manufacturers to enlist the services of the best designers of the day once more. Great interest was generated in home decoration, fashion and general creativity, and a wide range of wallcoverings were available using newly obtainable materials, including vinyls and washables, as well as cork, hessian and photographic murals.

The affluent young and socially mobile sought to reflect their somewhat easy-going lifestyles with products that were easy to maintain: laminated plastics imitating wood or marble were developed, and synthetic fabrics used widely. The schemes that proliferated were a curious blend of Modernism and Arts and Crafts styles. Wallpaper patterns were large, dominant and colourful.

Age of Co-ordination

The next two decades heralded a change in the English wallpaper industry for the concept of co-ordination, already extremely popular in America, reached the British industry. Manufacturers found increasing reliance on retailers instead of the decorating trade, through which they traditionally reached the general public. Sanderson, for example, refurbished its

London showroom into a retail store, where their collections introduced the relatively new concept of total co-ordination of wallpapers and fabrics. (The company had, however, matched cretonnes – heavy furnishing fabrics – to wallpapers since 1899, albeit informally.)

Retail divisions of other manufacturers soon followed their lead, offering the co-ordinated package that was to prove so popular into the 1990s: From just one outlet, customers could select wallpapers, curtain and upholstery fabrics, carpets, paints and accessories in mixed or matched ranges. The whole gamut of design styles could be offered, including pretty florals, finely detailed paisley patterns, elegant formal stripes, and bold Morris-inspired patterns. *Trompe l'oeil* borders, swags and accessories were offered to embellish ranges of background papers.

Into the Future

Fashion in interior design, as previously discussed, is cyclical, and many distinct styles in wallcoverings have seen service several times around since their original introduction. However, subtle changes usually differentiate each period of popularity whether in choice of colourways or stylistic nuances. While the logic of computer-aided design offers its own high-tech brand of graphics, traditional designs have an enduring popularity.

In 1990, for example, the popular artist Glyn Boyd Harte set out to revive the tradition of the artist craftsman with the release of a range of wallpapers and fabrics under the Dolphin Studio label. The beautiful designs – mainly lifesize depictions of flowers such as pansies and anemonies in their natural colours, with shading to make them appear three-dimensional – were produced by Boyd Harte drawing each colour separation himself. An exacting method that eliminates any mechanical preparation process prior to dye being applied to the paper or cloth, the finished result retains the character of the original and the hand of the artist. Dolphin Studio, although initially concentrating on the work of Boyd Harte, plans to commission designs from other well-known artists for future collections.

History, then, has witnessed the development of wallpapers from the rich designs reminiscent of mysterious, far-off lands, through its ability to mimic or simulate other, more exotic materials, its qualities that can echo the artistic skill of the designer, to the universal availability that mechanisation has brought. Styles have been sober, sombre, exuberant, flamboyant, images revivalist or futuristic. Late in the twentieth century, wallpaper design seems to have come full circle and it is difficult to foresee developments that can be regarded as truly original. But however it develops, despite its ever-changing face, it seems likely that the ubiquitous printed roll will endure into the next century.

A scattering of delicate anemones on a pale, plain background appear to float gently downward, creating a light, airy feel to artist Glyn Boyd Harte's own sunny bathroom.

FLOUR

CHAPTER THREE

COLOUR, TEXTURE AND PATTERN

Colour, texture and pattern each play an important role in a decorative scheme, the success of which lies in your skill in using them – alone or in conjunction with each other. Understanding the basic qualities of these elements is the first step in creating the effect you want.

Selecting colours to use in decorating is largely a matter of personal preference but, while there are no hard and fast rules when it comes to choosing, there are some basic guidelines of which you should be aware.

Colour Make-up

All colours are derived from three 'pure', or primary, colours – red, blue and yellow. Imagine each as the spoke of a wheel. When two of these colours are mixed in equal proportions, a secondary colour is formed: in this way, red plus blue makes violet; blue plus yellow makes green; yellow plus red makes orange.

The secondary colour appears on the colour wheel between its constituent colours, and opposite the one primary colour that is not used in its make-up: green, for instance, sits opposite red. These colours are known as complementary colours. They are the most contrasting colours in the spectrum; their use in a decorative scheme is typically for vivid, dramatic effect.

Tertiary colours are formed by mixing a primary colour equally with one of its neighbouring secondary colours: for example, turquoise is formed when blue and green are mixed.

The completed colour wheel, then, is a simplified means of visualizng the relationships between basic primary, secondary and tertiary colours: in reality, however, each colour merges imperceptibly with its neighbour, giving infinite variation in tone. The warm colours, which we commonly associate with sunlight and fire – yellows, oranges and reds – are grouped along one side of the colour wheel; the cooler colours, which suggest water, sky and plants – the blues and greens – are grouped along the opposite side.

Colourful Moods

Certain colours evoke in us different moods, which are usually associated with the temperature they suggest: colours, therefore, are often described as being warm or cool. Rich reds, for example, help to create a cosy, warming environment, while pale blues can suggest a refreshingly cool ambience. To clearly illustrate the relationships between colours and how these can be employed to create particular atmospheres, it's useful to use a visual device called a colour wheel.

Saturated red, with an intricate floral pattern, creates a warm, cosy atmosphere in this country-style kitchen, enhancing the subtle wood tones of the units.

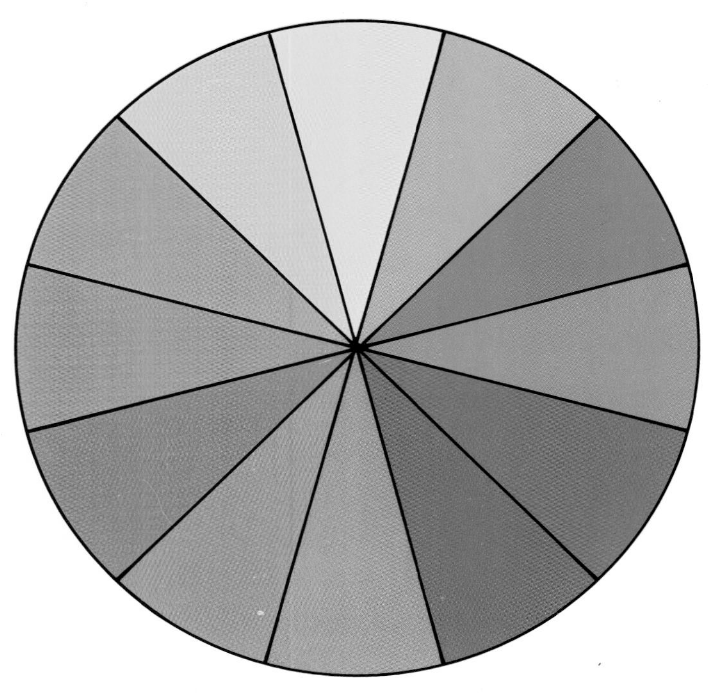

This basic colour wheel demonstrates the relationships between primary, secondary and tertiary colours: the warm and cool colours are grouped at opposite sides of the wheel; those directly opposite are known as complementary colours.

Tonal Qualities

Where subtlety is required in a decorative scheme, tints of purer colour are used. In its most basic form, different percentages of pure colour are used for a softer effect. However, it is also possible to alter a tone by adding a neutral. Neutrals are, in effect, not actual colours: black and white lack any pigment at all. When mixed together in varying percentages, black and white create innumerable tones of grey.

Neutrals alone do not clash with any other colour, but when small amounts of colour are added, they delicately assume the character of those colours. By adding white alone to a colour, pastel tones are formed which will blend with virtually any other colour; by adding black the shades become more enriched.

When all primary and secondary colours are mixed together, the colour brown is formed: here is a colour which is often used in the same way as a neutral, because it has elements which will, theoretically, blend with any other colour. With white or black added, brown, too, can also become a subtle tint or an even richer shade of colour.

Textural Touch

Texture is an ingredient in interior design that is just as important as the colours you may choose to use, and in fact it even has the ability to change the qualities of a colour. The effect of texture is primarily a tactile one – smooth, glossy woodwork feels cool to the touch, for

Swaying, intertwining grasses or licking flames – the imagination is fired by the richly textured surface of this Anaglypta vinyl wallcovering.

example, while a soft fabric wallcovering feels warm – but the visual appearance of texture also affects the mood and atmosphere of room decor to a great extent, if carefully chosen.

Light is reflected from a smooth surface, while rougher textures tend to absorb light, even to the extent that shadows are cast on the surface. Very smooth and very rough surfaces, however, are just the extremes: in between lies an infinite variety of textures.

Colour and Texture

A room scheme which used all the same texures for walls, floor, ceiling, furniture and furnishings would tend to be plain and uninteresting or else overpowering, depending on how smooth or rough the textures were. Therefore, it's best to use a combination of different textures in a single scheme to provide variety. Unlike mixing-and-matching colours, texures of a conflicting nature can be successfully used together without vying for attention. For example, contrast sumptuous, deep red, flock wallcovering with white-painted glossy doors, architraves and skirtings, offset by dark polished furniture and a velvet-pile carpet.

Textures on their own create distinctive effects but by adding colour you can also change the mood dramatically: the same colour added to both smooth and coarse textures will look entirely different. The coarseness of hessian, for instance, suggests a rich and warm texture; shiny metallic wallcoverings present a bright, cool, reflective surface; a plain matt surface absorbs light and gives a neutral background texture. Embossed wallcoverings give a regular, raised texture which you can paint matt or glossy, subduing or enhancing the impressed pattern respectively.

Pattern Effects

Pattern, whether abstract, naturalistic, random or symmetrical, is probably the most noticeable element in a decorative scheme, although its effect is transformed dramatically by the use of colour and texture. Although choice of patterns is largely a matter of personal preference and the effect you are trying to achieve, there are some points you should be aware of when selecting.

Large, dominant patterns will seldom contribute to a relaxed atmosphere; an arrangement of small motifs or a geometric design are more suitable. Mixing patterns calls for careful consideration to avoid a conflicting appearance, although you can co-ordinate a scheme by using the same pattern with different colourways, one for walls, the other for curtains.

Colour and pattern can be used to visually alter the proportions of a room. The warmer colours are said to advance and the cooler ones to recede. This means that a room painted with a strong emphasis on, say, red will appear smaller than if it was painted overall in a pale blue or green. You can use this optical illusion to improve the proportions and scale of an awkardly shaped room. For example, a high ceiling painted a dark tone will appear lower; treat the floor similarly and the room will appear smaller. Use the same technique to draw in the walls of a large room, or, with cooler colours, to visually expand a small space. Lighter tones used in a dark, narrow hallway will appear to push the walls outwards.

Patterns have a similar effect: horizontal stripes, for instance, will make a wall appear to be wider than it really is, while vertical stripes tend to visually increase the height of a room. Large, dominant patterns advance in the same way as plain, warm colours; small patterns do the opposite. On a large wall, small patterns will appear indistinct, more like an overall texture.

High contrast in a blaze of vivid colour, yet co-ordinated with a dense background paper hand-printed with fern motifs and opposite colourways used for curtains.

CHAPTER FOUR

CREATING ATMOSPHERE

When you are conversant with the basic principles of colour, texture and pattern, you can use what you have learnt to create characteristic mood with wallcoverings. Whether you want to evoke an atmosphere of rustic charms, an environment of period authenticity or sophisticated opulence, or a statement of slick modernity, you will find a wallcovering to suit.

Richly Decadent

Pale pastel colours may well be acceptable for a light, airy living room but are just too lightweight and fey for use in a hideaway bedroom or small, cosy sitting room, where you plan to retreat from the pressures of the day and unwind. Here you need visually weighty, cloyingly thick and deep colours to shroud you while you loll on the bed, or slouch in an easy chair with an engrossing book.

Red is the perfect colour for this sumptuous environment, and it's always evocative of a sense of well-being and relaxing warmth – yet blatantly decadent in the same instance.

To stand up to the confident depth of colour used for the background wallpaper, you will need to use equally rich colours – plump greens, deep pinks, thick yellows – for friezes, borders and dados. These features will only serve to enhance the colour and overall effect of the wallpaper. You should then introduce softer textures in the way of curtain fabrics, bedlinen and furniture upholstery – again, in bold colours – as a means of blending the various disparate aspects of the scheme.

Accessorize with gilt-framed pictures on the walls, silver or gold trinket boxes, glistening cut glass cosmetic bottles and vials. Keep artificial lighting to a moody minimum and filter daylight through translucent drapes overlaid with thick lined curtains.

The saturated red wallpaper of this bedroom creates an air of warmth infused with a touch of decadence. The adjoining dressing room virtually drips with the same intensity.

Rustic Charm

The archetypal country cottage, with its mass of exposed oak beams, low sagging ceilings and bulging plaster walls will perplex the prospective paperer. Ingenuity and sensitive choice of pattern and colour are needed.

The rural, unsophisticated charm of the English country cottage is frequently lost by insensitive treatments. Renovations intent on straightening up the crooked walls, smoothing out the bowed ceilings and concealing the rugged beams with flat plasterboad only serve to strip the cottage of quaint character.

All this 'modernization' is unnecessary, both aesthetically and from a practical viewpoint. Despite the standardized form in which wallcoverings are sold – many types of wallpaper are eminently suited to coping with irregular surfaces and awkward crevices.

What is important is a choice of pattern and colour that enhances the time-worn surfaces rather than competing with them, or concealing them. Small delicate patterns of an organic form are far more attuned to cottage character than geometric designs. Patterns should have as small a repeat as possible. By choosing this particular type of pattern, lengths can then be matched more easily at each side of a beam, and waste will be minimal. Cut the paper to follow the wayward contours of protruding timbers.

For a more random, or less contrived, effect choose wallcoverings with a finish that imitates the patina of distressed paintwork, or special paint effects such as sponging, dragging or rag-rolling. Papers with comparatively large plain areas, decorated with small flora, stencil-style motifs give a clean, fresh appearance that acts as a foil for a proliferation of exposed timberwork. By using these papers, pattern-matching is much less of a problem.

Pale blue paper and small busy floral motifs complement the irregular lines of the typical country cottage, especially when cut to fit round exposed, gnarled oak beams.

Sophisticated Opulence

A room of grandiose or elegant disposition, containing antique furniture amid plush furnishings, deserves an exuberant backdrop that flaunts its opulence. Be bold, exude a confident, luxurious air, but never be brash.

The amply proportioned drawing rooms of Victorian houses, and the genteel elegance of Georgian homes provide the perfect setting for treasured possessions, heirlooms and fine antiques – but a blatantly opulent atmosphere will be cheapened by poor choice in decoration for the walls. What is needed is a blend of pattern and colour that both reflects and accentuates the richness of the room's polished furniture, gilt-framed portraits, and assorted *objets*.

For example, consider the sheer extravagance of fabric wallcoverings such as the watered-silk effect of moiré, the delicate pile of suede, or the coarser depth of tweed. Each will give texture to walls (which must be flat, perfectly sound and unlikely to receive undue wear), but texture to feast the eyes only, for these are wallcoverings to sit back and admire – and touching is strictly forbidden. If, however, your vision of opulence is not backed up by vast funds – and expensive fabrics are beyond your budget – you can still simulate the effect with cheaper papers impressed with the patterns of woven fabrics.

Flocks with elaborate raised-pile patterns, and papers with vivid, bold designs will give an exotic effect, particularly when displayed in colourways of green, peacock blue, terracotta, fiery red and gleaming gold.

The sheer extravagance of watered silk moiré wallcovering makes the ideal backdrop for a room of unabashed flamboyance, furnished with thick damask drapes and adorned with assorted puttee and classical ornamentation.

Sleek and Stylish

Let the modern city apartment mirror the vitality of its bustling surroundings with vibrant abstract designs and clean, crisp colours.

The frantic, social whirl of the city dweller leaves little time for sinking into a sumptuous sofa and snoozing – that way you would miss all the fun – so reserve the soft touches for the bedroom and infuse your living and entertaining areas with a slick, eager atmosphere.

Hark back to the 1930s Modernist movement in interior design for inspiration – in those days many people could not take the austerity of the schemes, but now they are a perfect backdrop for the urban environment. However, pep up the usual subdued tones with cleaner, crisper colours: keep walls fairly plain and colours pure, with a bright primary border forming panels on the walls, or snaking around the room as a mock picture or dado rail. Hang bright, modern paintings of abstract style in geometric arrangements, or opt for a single huge painting dominating a wall with the panelled wallcovering as a frame.

If you would like to introduce pattern into the scheme, keep it subtle or it is likely to detract from the ascetic air you are aiming for. Choose a slim vertical pinstripe paper for all the walls: from close-up it is finely detailed, from afar it gives a pleasant glow of colour.

Furnish with slim-legged chairs in plain grey metal, glass-topped metal-framed occasional tables, and perhaps a matching *chaise* to lend much-needed horizontality to a largely geometric scheme.

Jaunty blue denim used on the walls of this sleek modern interior, is accentuated by candy-coloured upholstery and plain, uncluttered furniture and accessories.

Classic Elegance

Unassuming and dapper decor for the elegantly proportioned room demonstrates a confident yet quiet appreciation of classic designs.

Wallpaper need not be used forcefully to be effective. Economic use of colour, pattern and texture can be employed to enhance the shape, size and aspect of a room of fine proportion, such as the elegant symmetry found in Regency houses.

Decor should be similarly light of touch, using vertical pinstripes, broad stripes, small graphically drawn star or spot motifs with plenty of space around hem, tiny *fleurs de lys* on a plain background, or arranged geometrically within toning stripes over the surface of the wallcovering. Floral motifs, where favoured, should be two-dimensional and geometrically arranged, in the French provincial style.

Background colours are best kept muted – pale, misty, marbled or sponged yellows, greens or pinks – or deeper tones of these colours (but not heavy-handed), with the patterns coloured in neutrals, silver or gold.

Fabric drapes might complement the colouring of the wallcovering with pretty floral patterns in glazed cotton, or swirling foliage on a light background colour: they should, however, merely frame a window without transforming it into a dominant feature that detracts from the overall fresh, cool approach of the scheme.

Furnish with delicate, uncomplicated Regency-style furniture, upholstered sofas in plain, light fabrics, or coloured stripes, adorned with pretty Oriental cushions. Paintwork – doors, architraves, mouldings – should be white gloss by preference, or stripped and polished a subtle honey-tone.

Formal elegance in a Regency drawing room, with a subdued vertical stripe wallpaper and stylised flower motif. The fine lines of the furniture are contrasted with coarse-woven upholstery for texture.

Country Colour

Steeped in the patina of time, the faded but not jaded interior of the English country manor house, with its well-worn upholstery, accumulation of heirlooms and mementos from travels abroad, has an uncontrived lived-in look.

The quintessential English manor house interior, adored by British and foreigners alike, is not attainable merely by judicious use of paper and fabrics, or by 'acessorizing' accordingly. It is the result (although not the final outcome) of many years, even centuries, of residence. The heirlooms, mementos collected during travels far and wide, the family portraits adorning the walls, are not merely the ornamentation of a room, but part and parcel of its make-up. Fine furniture, now well-worn, is not for show but to be used; likewise, dusty drapes at windows, although once crisp, are now soft and faded. In short, the manor house is a continuing picture of history.

Copying the effect, or simulating it, requires considerable rethinking of the usual ideals of decorating, for the purpose is not to create a new-looking room but one that shows the signs of age. Like most decorative schemes the treatment of the walls is of utmost importance, for it will dictate the success or failure of the finished room.

Dusky tones are the best choice when considering the overall colour scheme, for these appear faded by long exposure to the sun: think about yellows, pinks, greens and blues. Pattern is permitted, such as an overall stippled or dragged effect, but naturalistic motifs (blooms, foliage) are best reserved for chintz curtains and the upholstery of armchairs and sofas. For overall pattern, select a paper with a small, fine, classical motif, a verti-

Ribbons and bows tied with pretty bouquets form a delicate curtain around the walls of this country house bedroom, softening the exuberance of the French antique bed.

cal or diagonal arrangement of stylized flowers or heraldic symbols printed subtly on a plain ground with much air around so as not to draw in the walls.

The floor should ideally be stripped, stained dark and polished, then covered with ragged rugs. Fitted carpet should be soft of pile and tone, perhaps picking out an element of colour from the curtain fabrics. Furnish with a serene mix of comfortable, well-padded, upholstered armchairs piled with embroidered cushions, tall wing chairs at fireside, and occasional tables on which you can display a clutter of photographs and ornaments.

Intimate Co-ordinates

Wrap yourself in a cocoon of co-ordinate pastel colour and soothing pattern with wallpapers, fabrics and accessories designed to mix, match and present an intimate, unified atmosphere.

If you hate loose ends you will adore the comforting intimacy you can introduce to your rooms with clever co-ordinates. Create a totally cohesive scheme by selecting from the ranges of wallpapers, curtain fabrics, paper borders and accessories such as lampshades and bases, cushions and bedlinen, which are intended to be used in conjunction with one another. They share the same or toning colourways, while the same motifs might be used small on the walls, larger on the curtains, larger still on furnishing fabrics.

With other co-ordinates, the colourways might be reversed for wallpaper and fabrics,

Mixed-and-matched motifs in pastel colours are repeated on fabric, upholstery and wallcoverings in various sizes and guises to create an intimate scheme of co-ordination for a bright bedroom.

yet the link may still be obvious to the eye.

Plain, unpatterned fabrics or accessories are likely to pick out a dominant colour in their patterned wallpaper counterpart, or offer a contrast; striped paper for a dado, floral-patterned fabric for bedlinen, or geometric border papers might just as likely highlight a colour from the overall pattern used on the wallcovering to link otherwise disparate shapes in an overall happy marriage.

It is this unified image which – rendered in pretty pastels – invests such a scheme with a gentle, relaxing air that's perfect for bedrooms, yet ideally suited to sitting rooms and dining rooms alike.

Masterfully Moody

Rich, saturated colours; bold, brazen patterns, and heavy ornamentation typify the excesses of Victoriana. Few other treatments have the ability to evoke such dark and moody period authenticity.

The word co-ordination must have meant little to the Victorians, for they would happily mix diverse and wholly disparate patterns, colours and textures into an amalgam which was impossible to take in at one glance. This is not to denigrate these nineteenth-century show-offs – social one-upmanship was indeed one of their primary goals – for their confident schemes showed a brilliant sense of the dramatic.

Big, roomy spaces were needed to accommodate such rich schemes, as indeed they preferably are today. Only then can the size-

Sumptuous saturation of colour surrounds you as you bathe in this Victorian-style tub, the moody green-papered walls daubed with sponged blotches in vivid bark.

SPIKE

able swirling foliage patterns of typical wallcoverings be shown to their best advantage, and the dark colours used without appearing to shrink the walls.

Should you only have modest-sized rooms, it is possible to apply a toned-down, smaller-scale image of the era using less ornamentation, smaller-patterned yet still vivid wallpaper, say with a tight geometric pattern rather than organic scrolls and blooms.

In larger rooms, divide the wall in true Victorian fashion into the three areas – dado, filling and frieze – fitting replacement wood mouldings where these have been removed. Paint the dado a deep colour, or use an embossed paper, then apply a bold floral paper to the filling. The frieze should be plaster in complex acanthus leaf pattern, or an elaborate paper frieze with deep, gaudy colouring and organic motif.

Furniture, too, should be exuberantly ornamental, in mahogany or the black ebonized mahogany that became popular after Prince Albert's death. Cram Chinese porcelain into every available space around the room, and balance potted aspidistra, palms and other exotic hothouse plants atop *jardinières*. Keep lighting subdued, with gas-lamp style wall fittings and coloured glass domes dangling from chains around central pendants.

Playful Primaries

Playroom plans demand a bright, jolly mix of primary colours with practical, wipeable surfaces, for this is a room where appearances set the scene and creative play is encouraged.

Children relate the most to the bright, primary, colours adults usually try to tone down in their own somewhat sombre territory. But in the magical world of the playroom you can afford to throw caution aside and create a wonderland of gaudy animation, gaiety and unabashed fun. Kids' toys are generally coloured red, yellow, blue or green, and these set the scene for the entire treatment.

Subtlety is outlawed in the playroom, especially with regard to pattern. Enliven the scene with a riot of the outlined motifs that are based on favourite or classic cartoon characters, expressed in the pure colours of animated films. Avoid the entire scheme looking like an explosion in a paint factory by choosing co-ordinated collections of backing paper, chunky self-adhesive border prints, related fabrics for curtains, blinds and – if the kids' bedroom is adjoining – bedwear and bedlinen.

Cartoon colouring in a playroom decorated with primary-toned motifs repeated in friezes, curtains and accessories.

Encouraged by your children's fancies, you can allow Tom and Jerry free rein to perform cat-and-mouse battle across the walls of the room, while their antics are repeated like the frames of a cartoon film around the ceiling angle, skirting or dado in the form of a border print. More orderly scenes of gaily painted balloons can fly in diagonal formation across the walls, while confined within the geometric pattern of matching curtains. Colours are picked from the balloons and used to form a dado of vertical stripes, while a horizontal border of dancing teddy bears circuits the room, again linked in colour to the walls.

Choose a brightly coloured, plain carpet as foil to the excesses of energy that abound, but choose a colour that occurs in the overall scene as a visual link. Adorn chairs, tables, cupboards with cut-out characters from the wallcovering, stuck on and varnished over, or try painting your own designs.

Most wallcoverings intended for kids' rooms are sensible washables or vinyls, for the excitement of play often results in crayons and pen scribbles.

CHAPTER FIVE

TYPES OF WALLCOVERING

The term 'wallpaper' is commonly used generically to describe all manner of wall coverings, but it is largely a misnomer, for out of the vast range available, only a relatively small proportion are made from wood pulp.

Wallpaper Sizes A standard roll of wallpaper measures 10.5 m (11 yd) long × 530 mm (21 in) wide, although specials might be wider, narrower, longer or shorter. Where sizes differ from the standard, commonly available dimensions are given.

Machine-printed Papers Ordinary wallpaper is available printed with a vast range of patterns of every conceivable form, in every colourway imaginable. Most types are machine-printed, which gives consistent colouring and pattern-matching. The cheaper types have a tendency to over-stretch and tear when pasted.

Hand-printed Papers Hand-printed papers are more delicate, more costly and awkward to hang: susceptible to tearing when wet, they are sometimes difficult to pattern-match because the hand-printing process is not as accurate as machine-printing. Paste smears on the surface can cause stains, and the ink may run. Some types come with a selvedge which needs trimming off for accurate pattern-matching. Limit hand-printed papers to areas not exposed to wear or condensation.

Washable Papers Similar to ordinary printed papers, washable types are coated with a thin transparent glaze of PVA (polyvinylacetate) to give a surface that can be cleaned with a damp sponge (although vigorous scrubbing will damage the PVA layer). They come into their own in environments where there is likely to be condensation present, such as bathrooms and kitchens.

Vinyls Durable, washable vinyl wallcoverings ideal for steamy areas consist of a backing of paper or cotton coated with a layer of vinyl, on which the design is printed, and the colours and vinyl are then fused by heat. Many vinyls are ready-pasted, requiring only water to activate the adhesive for easy application (for full details see page 101). For unpasted types, fungicidal paste is required to avoid the problem of mould growing behind the impervious covering. This type of wallpaper is particularly for kitchens and bathrooms.

Expanded (Blown) Vinyls Expanded (Blown) Vinyls are thicker than ordinary vinyls and can offer a greater degree of durability and washability.

Foamed Polyethylene Coverings Foamed plastic coverings, which have no backing paper, are printed with colourful patterns and designs to create a lightweight wallcovering. Novamura is the most widely known of this kind of covering and is hung by pasting the wall instead of the covering as is more usual. Although washable, it is quite delicate and should only be used on areas not subject to wear.

Flocks The familiar raised velvety pile effect of flock wallcoverings is created by sticking synthetic or natural fibres (commonly silk or wool) to a paper backing. The textured pattern and plain backing are normally two-toned. Hanging is not easy, for paste smears will ruin a natural pile; however, viny flocks can be washed without damage (and some are ready-pasted for easier application).

Printed papers come in a vast range of colourways and patterns, featuring traditional bird-and-foliage motifs, picture papers which form a busy, if repetitive mural. Simple graphic symbols such as stars, or plain stripes. Border papers and trompe l'oeil *pieces complete an overall scheme.*

Foils Reflective foil wallcoverings comprise a paper backing coated with a metallized plastic film. They are usually sold in a range of contrasting textures, with a matt design printed over the foil in such a way that the reflective finish gleams through. Although they are ideal for small, dark rooms, foils tend to highlight uneven surfaces.

Hessian Paper-backed hessian, usually sold in 889 mm (35 in) or 914 mm (36 in) wide rolls, comes in several shades, and can be overpainted if required. Furnishing hessian comes in broad rolls, and is usually sold by the metre. Because it is unbacked and loose-woven, the condition and colour of the wall behind are crucial to a successful finish. Furnishing hessian should be colour-fast, shrink-resistant and moth-proof.

Felt and Suede Felt and imitation suede wall-coverings are usually paper-backed, heavyweight fabrics made from dyed compressed wool. Rolls are typically 700 mm (28 in) wide, making hanging tricky. The wall is pasted and the covering applied from the bottom up.

Grasscloth This material is made by weaving natural grasses with a fine cotton weft, which is then glued to a paper backing and sold in typically 914 mm (36 in) wide rolls. Not hardwearing, grass-cloth is fragile and difficult to hang: it is usual to paste the paper backing rather than the wall.

Fabrics Furnishing fabrics such as wool, tweed and silk can be used as a wallcovering for feature areas. Unbacked types can be stuck directly to the surface of a pasted wall; stapled to a series of battens fixed around the room, or fixed to lightweight panels which are then attached to the wall. Backed fabrics such as cotton, linen or silk come stuck to a paper backing for application to a smooth, flat surface.

Cork Coverings Thin veneers of natural or coloured cork stuck onto a paper backing give a textured wallcovering that is warm to the touch. Some types have a contrasting coloured backing, which shows through the cork in a random pattern.

Relief Coverings Heavyweight relief coverings, also called 'whites', have a deeply embossed pattern – usually classically sculptural or geometric – and are generally used for concealing minor surface imperfections and for over-painting. The most widely known type, Anaglypta, is embossed on both sides: two sheets of paper are bonded together, then passed between embossing rollers. Supaglypta is a stronger version made using cotton fibres instead of wood pulp, and will withstand much deeper embossing. Vinaglypta, made from vinyl, has the deepest embossing; heated in an oven the vinyl expands (or 'blows') embossing it.

Lincrusta is a heavy, embossed covering with a flat paper back. The raised pattern is made from a solid film of linseed oil and fillers fused onto a backing paper, and the pattern is then applied with an engraved steel roller. Sold in roll form, the edges and ends must be trimmed prior to hanging; in panel form, Lincrusta is used to make a dado. Lincrusta designs range from classic floral and foliage patterns to geometric effects and even tile, brick or wood simulations.

Ingrain Paper (Woodchip) A relief wallcovering used as a lining prior to painting the wall, ingrain or woodchip paper is coated with small chips of wood sandwiched between two layers of paper.

Lining Paper Used on bare walls prior to painting or hanging other decorative wallcoverings, lining paper gives a smooth, flat and uniform finish, concealing minor imperfections. When being used solely for painting, lining paper is hung vertically – just like ordinary wallpaper – but when used behind wallcoverings it is hung horizontally so that the butt joins will not show through the decorative surface.

Borders Border papers come in various widths from about 50 to 150 mm (2 to 6 in), and are printed with a pattern, which often complements a range of wallpapers. Use borders around the top of the walls as a frieze, above the skirting, at dado height, or to form 'panels' on a plain wall or previously papered surface.

Textured wallcoverings vary from basic woodchip backings through rich, delicate grasscloths, pressed leaf collages, suedes, corks, woven fabrics such as hessian, wool or glassfibre, to glittering metallic foils with a shiny smooth surface and bold printed pattern and embossed vinyl coverings.

CHAPTER SIX

ROLL CALL

Determining the atmosphere you want to conjure up is just the first step in creating a unique decorative scheme. With an inkling of the effects of colour, pattern and texture, now is the time to explore the host of wallcoverings available to find the particular properties that will bring your schemes to fruition.

The Wet Set

Durable vinyls and washables that excel in steamy bathrooms and kitchens . . .

Steam does not create the perfect environment for ordinary wallcoverings to remain stuck to the surface – in fact a steam stripper is often the tool used to remove unwanted wallpaper. In rooms such as kitchens where pans continually bubble and bathrooms where showers and capacious tubs of hot water exude a hot, misty atmosphere, special impervious coverings are required. Sensible precautions in reducing the formation of water vapour should also be taken.

Wallcoverings for steamy areas should ideally have insulating as well as water-resistant properties, so that wall surfaces can be kept as warm as possible to discourage moisture from forming. There are several suitable wallcoverings, notably the foamed polyethylene Novamura; relief papers such as blown vinyls and cork wallcoverings are also beneficial. Consider lining the walls with insulating polystyrene sheet prior to hanging the wallcoverings: this material, sold in rolls, bridges small holes and hairline cracks but dents easily and should not be used in areas that are likely to receive a lot of wear.

Highly unsuitable for steamy rooms are any type of fabric wallcoverings, grasscloths and flocks. Relief coverings are less suitable in kitchens, where grease deposits can collect in the emboss.

CONDENSATION CAUSES AND CURES

Understand how condensation forms and you will be able to eradicate it. 'Superficial' condensation is formed when warm moist air meets a cooler surface then loses its ability to hold the moisture when the temperature drops to dew-point. The result: water droplets deposited on surfaces, streaming down walls and windows, ruining decorations. Making the walls warmer with an insulating wallcovering will ease the problem. Additionally, fit lids on pans when cooking, run cold water before hot, and duct a tumble dryer outside to reduce the formation of water vapour. Stable room temperatures (via central heating), ventilation (via fans) and insulation of cold surfaces (via cavity wall insulation) will also help to eliminate condensation.

Versatile vinyls are vital in the steamy kitchen, yet designs need not be utilitarian, as this rambling foliage pattern proves.

BISCUITS

Billy's

Scribble Ability

Wipeable, washable wallcoverings that prove a match for crayon-wielding kids . . .

Where condensation is not a problem but where walls are prone to sporadic attack by juvenile grafitti artists, wipeable wallcoverings are indeed a boon. Vinyls again score top of the list for their durable, washable, often scrubbable qualities.

Lively patterns on papers typically discourage the scribbling urge by depicting cartoon characters and superheroes in frenzied action to keep the child's mind actively occupied. Colours are primary and bright.

Favourite colours are typically primary and always bright. Most children love reds, blues, yellows and vivid greens – the colours of cartoons – and these will all help to stimulate jolly, creative play.

Pick out certain colours from the wallcovering to use in curtains and other fabrics, or use co-ordinating ranges of fabrics and papers, which feature recurring motifs and patterns.

You might even consider cutting motifs from a spare roll of wallcovering and using them to decorate nursery furniture, sealing them with several coats of clear polyurethane varnish, *découpage* fashion.

In the kids' territory a wallcovering that can withstand sporadic scribbling will save constant redecorating. Children's papers come in jolly colours and patterns, often with matching friezes and border trims.

Where young scribblers are at large you don't necessarily need to paper the entire room from floor-to-ceiling with a wipeable, washable wallcovering: the prevailing stature of the juvenile offenders happily means they cannot reach to wield their crayons and pens more than a few feet above the ground.

The situation allows you to afix a practical vinyl wallcovering at dado level, where scribbles will not be a disaster, and to use a less practical, and possibly prettier ordinary printed paper above – safely out of reach. Make the dado deeper than it would normally be – about 1.2 m (4 ft) should be about right – to discourage outstretched arms from straying across the border. This option is sensible from a financial point of view, too, as plain printed papers are generally cheaper than vinyls.

For younger members of the family, nursery wallcoverings come in pretty pastel patterns – balloons, teddy bears and clowns – with matching borders and bedding to complete the co-ordinated look.

In short, vinyls are coverings that last, which will take some well-intentioned abuse. The heat-fused colours and vinyl layer assure permanent patterns and depth of colour.

PRE-PASTING PARTICULARS

Many vinyl wallcoverings are sold ready-pasted for easy application: all you do is cut the drops to length, roll up face inwards and dunk in a specially provided tray of water to activate the adhesive. Draw the end of the paper out of the tray, placed close against the skirting, and apply direct to the wall surface. Smooth in place with a damp sponge.

Tough Textures

Durable wallcoverings with unsurpassable depth of emboss for areas of heavy wear and tear . . .

The passage of time and changing decorative trends has done little to relax the popularity of one of the most durable embossed wallcoverings. Lauded for its intricacy of pattern and solid, permanent emboss, Lincrusta relief wallcovering – first developed in 1877 – is still available today in an original range of designs which span the decades since the first pattern – a bold swirl of foliage called *Italian Renaissance* – saw light of day in 1896.

Lincrusta, conceived by Frederick Walton, previously an employee of the Staines Linoleum company of Sunbury-on-Thames, has been manufactured since 1918 by Anaglypta's Queens Mills in Darwen, Lancashire, using the original brass rollers. Crown Decorative Products, who now produce the wallcovering, found they had to reintroduce the range of friezes, dados and roll wallcoverings due to strong popular demand and not just by owners of period properties, for the stylish patterns have proved to be ageless: the longevity of the product is evident by the number of originals that still adorn older homes to this day.

Lincrusta's designs evoke the prevalent styles of their day – a fact relished by the manufacturers, whose brochure lists the year each design was first introduced. There are a dozen roll patterns in the range, including the flamboyant foliage so popular during the late nineteenth century; the linenfold, bamboo lattice and waney oak designs from the 1950s and 1960s; geometric patterns from the 1970s; a pair of dados – Art Nouveau and Edwardian – from the early 1900s; six classical friezes devised between 1914 and 1920 and three borders.

The word Lincrusta comes from the Latin *linium* meaning 'flax' and *crusta* meaning 'rind'. Originally dubbed 'Linoleum Muralis', as a linoleum-type of wall decoration the basis of its composition is blown linseed oil, paraffin wax, whiting and resin. These are mixed in the correct proportions to create a cohesive compound which is then fused onto a heavy-duty backing paper. The design is then applied to the face by the use of a steel-engraved roller.

Processed rolls of Lincrusta are stored for two weeks under scrupulous conditions while the compound matures; this causes the relief texture to harden fully. Although it is fairly brittle if mishandled – and quite tricky to apply (see page 114) – once hung, the surface of the wallcovering is eminently tough and able to withstand considerable abrasion. The wallcovering, notably the dados in the range (see page 80), is used widely in areas of heavy traffic such as hallways and passages, whereas it can be quite dramatic as a means of decorating a sitting room, dining room or bedroom. This particular type of wallcovering is rarely found in kitchens, where grease would tend to collect in the heavily textured surface.

Lincrusta is certainly not the cheapest of wallpapers: one roll measuring 10.05 m (11 yd) will yield only three drops of an average height room. However, it is a good investment as it is hard wearing and requires minimal maintenance, needing only the occasional replacement coat of paint.

The finished effect of the Lincrusta depends on the type of paint you use to decorate it with. The manufacturers recommend an eggshell (semi-gloss) or oil-based high gloss paint for its durability, but you should be aware that the sheen will highlight the emboss greatly. If wearability is not important there is no reason why you should not decorate the Lincrusta with a matt-finish emulsion, which will tend to tone down the emboss.

'Italian Renaissance' from the Lincrusta range by Crown is a swirling mass of foliage, practical for use in a hallway, where it becomes a dramatic feature in its own right.

Raised Patterns

Relief wallcoverings with an embossed pattern that give richly textured character to a scheme . . .

The lasting appeal of embossed wallcoverings lies in their use of raised, textured designs rather than that of a flat, colour-printed pattern. Most relief coverings – or 'whites', as they're commonly known – are intended to be decorated with a matt or silk emulsion paint to complement or contrast with furnishings and other accessories. Colour is added as vividly or as subtly as takes your whim. Colour puts the final touch to relief coverings, suggesting a cool lightness or a rich, enveloping warmth.

Patterns are many and diverse: bold, writhing foliage and blossoming florals; sharp, zig-zagging geometrics; trickling watered-silk effects; coarse wedding-cake stucco; pitted lunar-landscape; formal stripes. The impact of the overall design, however, depends on the depth of the emboss, and this might be delicately understated or three-dimensionally loud and forceful. Choice requires some careful consideration.

Choose the random patterns of the very lightest of embosses, for instance, as a delicate backdrop for more vibrant soft furnishings, and use pastels for colour. Medium-weight embosses lend an air of refinement to traditional and modern settings, requiring an elegant touch in furniture and furnishings. Reserve the most deeply embossed wallcoverings for areas where greatest dramatic effect is called for, and where exemplary resilience is desirable. The high elevations of hallways and stairwells, for example, can take the boldness of a busy, deep relief wallcovering with a regular, formal pattern, while the softer, organic-based designs are eminently suited to the bed-

Soft options for an intimate bedroom with an embossed vinyl wallcovering – coloured in two tones of blue – in swirling textured pattern reminiscent of flowing silken drapes.

room or relaxation of a cosy sitting room.

Examine the quality of the emboss carefully when choosing your raised pattern design, for although many of them are crush-proof, just as many are not.

Not all relief wallcoverings, however, are meant to be overpainted. There are a good many pre-finished, high-relief textured vinyls available, which incorporate the durability of whites such as Anaglypta with the colouring of ordinary printed papers. Colour is commonly applied to the flat vinyl backing and the blown or foamed emboss overlaid, giving a subtle depth to the design.

Shining Examples

Reflective wallcoverings and subtle lighting work together to create a dramatically illuminated environment . . .

Shining wallcoverings can be infused with delicate veins of silver, overprinted with colourful florals, or silver or gold threads weaving in and out of geometric patterns, all opulent and showy. Foils rely on the play of natural and artificial light on their highly reflective surfaces to bring about a vibrant, ever-changing image. Move your gaze across the so-flat surface of a foil paper and the image will appear to change before your eyes.

With some foils, the entire backing paper is metallized and reflective, with the matt pattern printed on top. These highly reflective types act just like a mirror, and are excellent for dark rooms such as bathrooms and WCs, which might have little or no natural illumination; a single light bulb will bring the foil immediately to life. A perfectly flat wall, free from imperfections, is a prerequisite for all-over foils, for any defects will be vividly highlighted by the thin, shiny surface.

This is not to say that all foils are brash and glitzy, although undoubtedly some are. Sympathetic lighting and sensible choice of location are essential to prevent these characterful foils from swamping a room scheme.

Reflective thoughts in a dimly lit bathroom without natural light: the artificial illumination creates a glamorous glow on the shining foil wallcovering.

In daylight, foils may assume a silvery hue; under the glare of a lamp they might become more enriched. Overprinted with plain colour, the shiny parts of the design will advance when strong light is bounced from their glitter-like (magnified) surface, yet recede in dimmer light, appearing to thrust the colour forward. In certain lighting conditions, parts printed with the metallized plastic coating can even appear to disappear, transforming the wall-covering from its dominant role to an altogether more subtle approach.

Not all shiny wallcoverings are metalized foils, however: vinyls have an inherent sheen, which strong light can make more pronounced. Relief vinyls are impressed with a pattern, the various parts of which catch the light in different ways to either throw the pattern into glistening relief or make it appear flat and matt.

LEVELLING A WALL

Reflective wallcoverings will highlight an uneven or patched surface so it is advisable to level a significantly uneven wall to give a perfectly flat base. Screw slim softwood battens horizontally to the wall at 300 mm (12 in) intervals. Check with a spirit level that the wall battens are flat, and pack out behind any low ones with offcuts of hardboard. Cut panels of plasterboard to fit over the battens, butt-jointed at the edges, then attach to the battens with plasterboard nails. Seal the joins between the panels with special filler and paper tape 'scrim'. When dry, you can hang the wallcovering confident that the surface is flat.

Soft Options

Using the mellow, tactile qualities of fabrics to convey a richly coloured atmosphere . . .

The soothing, enveloping qualities of walls draped with finely woven fabrics such as silk cloth and suede are perhaps an extravagance most people would consider reserving only for rooms regarded as special – a sumptuous dining room, for example, or a luxurious bedroom where an atmosphere of restful calm is desirable. Their considerable expense notwithstanding, most fine fabrics are difficult to clean, susceptible to moist atmospheres, and act like a sponge for the odours from cooking.

However, used with imagination, their colours, patterns and textures can create a link with the type of mood and atmosphere you want to convey. For example, the woollen textures of tweeds and rich, colourful tartans are reflective of the country manor setting. The fine, soft pile of imitation suede with a pale yellow tone can be successfully linked to the theme of a desert of rolling sand dunes, and the room furnished as if a grand tent.

Silks and fine watered fabrics possess a feel of opulence that is best matched to fine antiques, and colourful porcelain vases from the East. Powder blues and emerald greens give a cool, light air to a room, while heavy, thick-pile damask curtains provide a contrast to the delicate sheen of the finer fabrics.

Coarse textiles such as hessian can add a strong tactile impression which softens the severity of a room. Opt for an architectonic environment with brown-coloured hessian against white paintwork. Furnish with natural wood furniture, varnished and honey-toned, or make use of plywood to create furniture and units with contrasting plain surfaces.

Highly coloured glazed chintz on the walls of this bedroom gives a subtly soft texture to the surface, and is used on curtains and upholstery for unity.

Padded Surfaces

Swaddle yourself in reams of fabric by creating your personal retreat from reality . . .

Fabric wallcoverings certainly serve to soften the inherent harshness and solidity of plasterwork, and you can enhance the atmosphere still further by creating walls that actually feel softly padded. Rather than sticking the fabrics to the surface, where the hardness of the walls is still detectable to the touch, consider covering the surface with fabric over a squashable padding that will not only absorb sound in the room (itself creating an eery effect), but also help to insulate the surface, keeping the room significantly warmer and cosier.

In the fashion of early householders, stretch fabrics over slim wooden frameworks and screw to the surface of the wall; add a padding of fire-retardent polyester wadding to the wall behind the fabric so that the surface is soft to the touch. You could even consider quilting the fabric for a more three-dimensional finish.

TENTING A CEILING

Complete a tented effect with fabric used on the walls by draping the ceiling with fabric, too. While there is no reason why you should not attach fabric-stretched panels to the ceiling in the same way as for the walls, a more sumptuous effect can be created by allowing the fabric to hang from fixed points in dramatic folds. For example, a circular rail attached to the centre of the ceiling, with handsome pendant light or chandelier dangling from the middle, can be hung with swags of fabric taken and fixed to the ceiling and wall angle, and left hanging in voluminous folds like an oriental tent.

Alternatively, drape the fabric over lengths of dowel or cornice poles fixed near the ceiling, so that the material billows between.

Soft, padded walls deaden sound in a room, while creating a delicately textured surface. Deep red accentuates the warmth.

An alternative padded effect can be created by stretching fabric over an inherently soft man-made board such as fibreboard: although rigid, the board is quite spongy when prodded (too much prodding, however, will damage it!). Secure the fabric with staples (see the instructions on page 119) and attach the panels directly to the wall surface with wallboard adhesive, or else screw them on. Leave the butt-joins between the fabric-covered panels uncovered to emphasize their shape, or conceal the joins with braiding stuck over them.

A curtained effect can be created by tenting the walls of the room with loosely hung fabrics. Battens slotted into hems at top and bottom of the 'curtains' are fixed to the wall to keep the fabric fairly taut – yet you'll be able to part it for easy access to light switches and other concealed fixtures, or merely to reveal a section of wall painted to complement the colour and pattern of the fabric. For example, draw the drapes of fabric back slightly from the centre of the wall, in neat folds or pleats, like the curtains on a stage, and stand a favourite ornament – say a statuette or vase of flowers – on a column: lit from behind by uplighters or downlighters, the wall will itself resemble a stage with the show about to commence.

Generous curtaining creates the illusion of a desert tent, where pleated drapes are hung between floor and ceiling, covering plain, less-than perfect plasterwork.

WALL UPHOLSTERY SYSTEM

Proprietary wall upholstery kits are available, with which you can apply fabric in the form of vertical or horizontal panels to walls or ceilings. The basis of one easily-available kit from America is the plastic track used to attach the fabric to the wall.

First, the lengths of track are fixed to the wall to form the perimeter of the panels. Adjoining panels are butted together to complete an entire area. After peeling off the protective backing, the track can be pressed into place using its adhesive backing; heavy-duty staples complete the fixing. The track is taken around wall switches, socket outlets, doors and windows.

The fabric is cut to the size of the panels, plus a margin of about 25 mm (1 in) all round. Insert the margin of fabric into the track's channel, starting at the top left corner and working down the left side. Snap the track shut to retain it. Stretching the fabric across the panel, insert the margin in the top track and snap it shut. Insert in the right side of the track, keeping the fabric taut, and finally retain in the bottom edge of the track.

Adjoining panels are completed in the same way. There will be a slight gap between panels, in which you can slide a narrow strip of fabric to fill; similar gaps at internal corners, where panels adjoin, can be filled with tight welts (rolls) of fabric slid between the channels, which produces a rounded profile.

To give a padded, truly upholstered surface, cut polyester wadding to fit within the panels prior to attaching the cover fabric.

Tenting a Ceiling

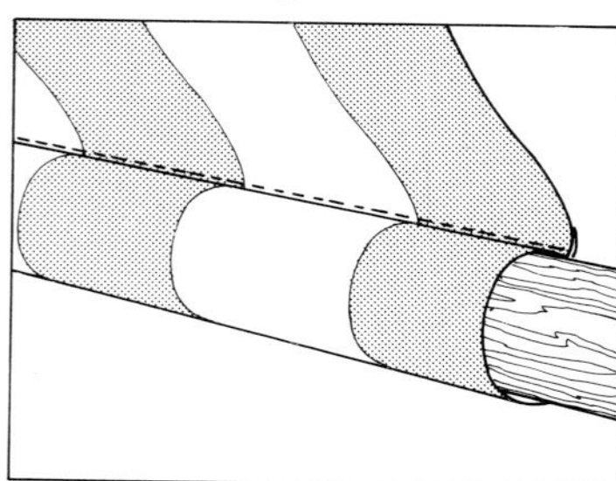

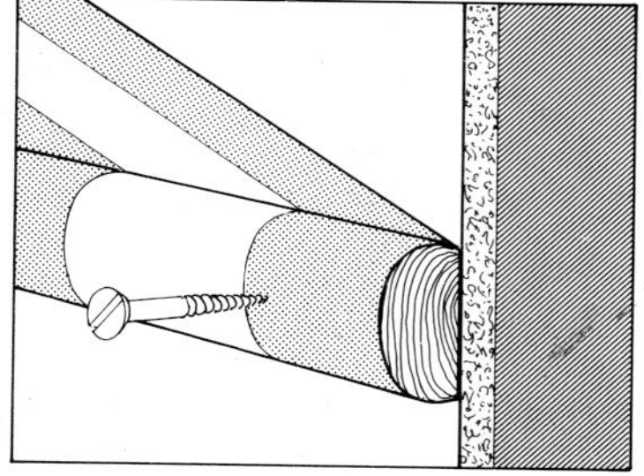

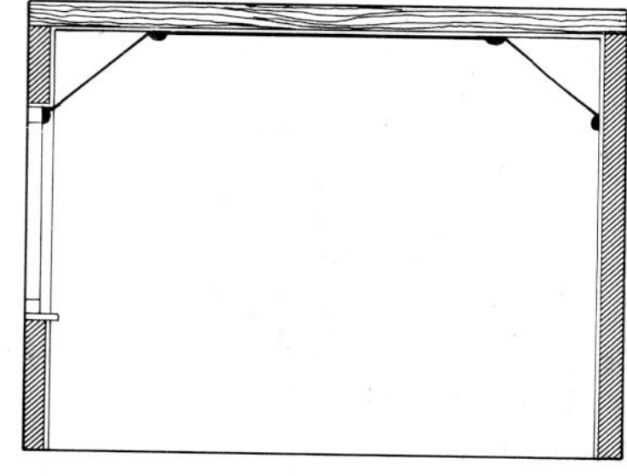

First wind fabric round a batten and sew securely underneath (1). The batten was then screwed to a joist on the left-hand ceiling side, leaving overlap. The fabric was then wound to another batten and stapled, then stretched tightly across and screwed to a joist on the right-hand side of the ceiling, again leaving overlap. Remaining fabric on the left-hand side was wound round another batten screwed to the window frame. Finally right-hand side excess fabric was wound round a batten and fixed to the wall. Trim with fringed fabric secured with adhesive tape on the undersides.

Tactile Patterns

Dark, luxuriant flock papers drenched with colour ideally suit a sumptuous setting . . .

Flocked paper, with its distinctive raised pattern, was originally devised as a cheaper alternative to the fabric hangings that adorned the walls of early, wealthy homes. Elaborately patterned, opulent flocked papers with designs of Eastern influence were typically saturated in rich tones of red, brown, purple or blue, on a contrasting or toning background. They were supremely common in homes of the late nineteenth century, where they formed an essential part of an overall scheme that could at times be justifiably described as a riot of pattern, colour and texture.

Soft-piled though it is, flock demands unabashed boldness in its application: you can never give it enough room to flaunt its confident character. Spacious parlours, formal dining rooms, luxurious bedrooms, each call for overall treatment with flock wallcovering, counterbalanced with either a similarly boldly marked carpet or, if plain, one in a toning colour and deep pile. Thick fabric drapes and upholstery with deep texture and rich colour, a profusion of strong pictures in heavy frames will be a necessity to break up the dominating influence of this paper. Allow the flock to dominate, however, in smaller rooms such as WCs, where the combination of large, tactile pattern and deep colouring creates a warmth all of its own.

Should you wish to you can tame the wilder tendencies of flocked paper by containing it within the confines of a dado and picture rail, with the area below and that above (including the ceiling) treated more plainly, yet certainly not subtly. This treatment suits a regal hallway and broad stairway, where ornate wall lamps enrich the colouring by casting pools of light on the fine raised pile. Use flock to decorate inside moulded wooden framing applied to large, flat walls, contrasting it with a lighter overall colour or regular pinstripe pattern. Here, the flock is used to create areas of rich texture within otherwise plain surfaces; an ornate wall light fixed in the centre of the frame will highlight the pile of the flock to its greatest advantage.

Exotic Emphasis

Fine, woven grasses which evoke the exotic atmosphere of the Orient . . .

Of all the wallcoverings we can choose to adorn our rooms, only the finely woven grasscloth can create the atmosphere of distant lands and temperate climates. Fragile in appearance and brittle to the touch, grasscloth wallcoverings invest a delicacy to elegant rooms. No ordinary wallcoverings, these require great care in application, considerable care in maintaining their lovely appearance, and sensitivity when complementing with other furnishings.

Colours are always subdued, natural tones, while single strands are frequently unevenly coloured: popular tones include straw yellows, pinks, pale buffs, dusty greens and smokey greys. The thickness of the individual strands

Sumptuously decadent surroundings suggested by the soft textures of flocked wallcovering in this Russian-style bedroom with four-poster drapes in matching thick damask.

woven into the cotton weft vary and are irregular. Some are thin fronds, others comparatively fatter, rounder lengths, while still others are flat slivers; the stalks of some show offshoots where blades of grass once grew, while the weft itself is often ragged, contributing to the hand-woven appearance of the wallcoverings.

Present a unified scheme with furniture made from rattan or light wood, chairs with rush or cane seats, glass-topped tables to reflect the surroundings. Fill the room with large potted palms and other exotic plants, cover the windows with fine net or wooden slatted venetian blinds which can filter the sunlight in varying degrees.

Cork Combinations

Tactile, richly coloured and random-patterned, cork has a comforting warmth . . .

As a wallcovering that combines rugged good looks with a measure of practicality, cork reigns supreme. Its touch is hard yet softly yielding, and it has useful insulating properties.

Cork, supplied in roll form and usually paper-backed and fairly thin, looks much more solid that it really is. Its random pattern, formed by a compression of fragments that range in tone from pale browns through reds, pinks, dark browns and even black, means that each scheme is unique. Artificially coloured cork increases the versatility of the wallcovering still further.

Patterns in cork vary immensely: in some, the cork fragments are quite sizeable, curving slivers, arranged in rivulets that run vertically down the covering; with others, the cork is composed of speckled chunks squashed into a cohesive surface.

With paper-backed types, the backing often shows through the many holes in the thin slivers of cork stuck to its surface. It is usually coloured to contrast with the tone of the cork, creating an impression of depth.

Cork coverings excel in bathrooms, where the insulating surface they create discourages condensation from forming. In artificial light – especially in a windowless bathroom – the cork surface appears rich and textural. In other rooms, the irregular patterning of the cork-covered paper can be counterbalanced with shiny chromium-framed furniture, glazed surfaces, or plain, pale colours and slim-framed chairs and tables.

The delicate Oriental look is evoked by the use of a grasscloth or reeded wallcovering, which consists of fine strands of dried grasses or slivers of cane, arranged side-by-side, woven together and stuck to a paper backing.

Cork, soft yet firm, gives a supremely tactile wall surface that is also thermally insulating. Leave it in its natural honey-tone, or paint as required.

Hand Block-Printed Patterns

Traditional hand block-printed wallcoverings that bear the hallmark of the artist's skill...

Before the age of the continuous paper-printing machine, all papers were hand printed using wooden blocks, sometimes with thick lino fixed to the surface to take the carved design. Many of these blocks survive to this day – notably those by William Morris – held in the archives of wallpaper manufacturers or historians.

Specialist companies and enterprising individuals offer papers printed from original blocks by traditional methods – and the results, although considerably more costly than machined types, are infinitely truer to the designer's original concept, more closely representing his or her artistic abilities. Hand-printed papers have an innocent simplicity in their representation: unchecked by today's modern and accurate production methods, rolls can be of variable printing quality and pattern-matching can be difficult.

The dyes used in the production of hand-printed papers tend to run if smeared with paste, so hanging demands considerable care. The papers themselves can stretch substantially and tend to tear easily when wet.

Although new blocks are frequently made to replace old worn types, many modern hand-printed papers tend not to be printed using the somewhat cumbersome wooden blocks. Instead, they are produced by the screen-printing method, which gives the same desired artistic eccentricities as the block method, but which is less labour-intensive.

Some complex block-printed designs required in excess of a dozen separate blocks: as each colour had to be dried prior to the application of the subsequent colour, and each block separately mounted and accurately positioned, the job was clearly laborious.

Often patterns originally printed by blocks have been translated as screen designs, which enables old-style wallpapers to be reproduced even when the original wooden blocks have been lost, destroyed or damaged beyond repair.

Block-printed patterns come into their own when organic motifs are expressed rather than geometric designs: swirling foliage, blossoming flowers, rambling woody stems or sheaves of corn swaying in the breeze. Motifs may well be repeated along the length of a paper, yet they are repeats that are not identical: instead, they contain those subtle 'inaccuracies' that make them so original.

Because of their high cost and vulnerable nature, it is probably best to reserve hand-printed papers for feature walls that will not be subjected to undue wear. Avoid cluttering the surface with too many pictures or furniture: appreciate these papers as the works of art that they are.

Arts and Crafts style in a hand-blocked printed wallcovering that demonstrates the innocent representation of the artist's hand at work.

CHAPTER SEVEN

ILLUSIONS OF GRANDEUR

Evoke the atmosphere of a crumbling Baroque villa, or the romantic impression of a tented desert camp with extravagant* trompe l'oeil *effects that come as paste-on cut-outs to transform a dull, flat surface into a fabulous mirage.

Paper Pillars

Flamboyant architectural details of a Classical era that fool the eye . . .

The excesses of the Baroque period of architecture which swept through Europe during the late sixteenth to early eighteenth centuries were characterized by heavily ornamented fluted columns, plaster bas-reliefs depicting fauns and other figures and furbelows. However, not all citizens could afford the full splendour of these fanciful ornaments, and came to rely on fakery to keep up social appearances.

Trompe l'oeil – literally 'to deceive the eye' – evolved as a technique to visually enlarge spaces and to create illusions of grandeur on flat, plain walls and ceilings. While exponents of decorative painting still abound, their services can be prohibitively expensive – it is essentially a work of fine art. Enterprising wallpaper manufacturers and specialist companies, however, offer collections of original hand-painted *trompe l'oeils*, reproduced to high technical standards, which are available as pre-cut portions for easy application to your walls. Colourings are subtle, yet the paper pieces appear hard and stone-cold.

Exercise your imagination to create a vista beyond the confines of your room's four walls. Start with the basic overall colour scheme of the wall: the illusion is best applied to a fairly plain surface. This may be a distant landscape painted onto lining paper or a two-tone representation of sky and land with little realistic detail. Alternatively, use one of the many interesting paint-effect papers available as a backdrop on which you can place the *trompe l'oeil* pieces, which can be stuck on with ordinary wallpaper adhesive.

Sold singly or in packs, the components can be assembled to create lofty floor-to-ceiling columns – typically topped with the curling foliage of Corinthian capitals, or the comparatively plainer Ionic style. Or you can use the broken, crumbling *trompe l'oeil* columns to create a scene of decadent ruin at floor level.

To be effectively convincing, small rooms can sensibly accommodate only two full-size columns, although with larger spaces columns can be 'erected' at each corner, and intermediate columns spaced between. Paint the ceiling a sky blue to suggest an open-air atrium, or use streaky grey to suggest a stone

The vista beyond brought into focus with a panoramic scene formed by a sectional printed mural, with cut-out trompe l'oeil *columns and balustrade stuck on top.*

roof supported by columns. An entire stone-look balustrade can be assembled using *trompe l'oeil* balusters, rails and supports, running the width of a wall between columns, or rising regally up a staircase from the hall.

Other features available to complete the ornamentation of your vision include busts and statues in classical pose, arched alcoves, urns – even rows of books that tempt you to pick them up and leaf through the pages.

Fabric Façades

Voluminous drapes that soften a scheme with opulent elegance . . .

While Baroque-style *trompe l'oeil* features are commonly used in misty tones of grey reminiscent of faded marble or plaster, a softer, yet more colourful, image can be created from the ranges of *trompe l'oeil*-effect components that simulate the appearance of grand swags of material. As well as yards of fake fabrics, you can choose from a selection of complex silky bows, delicately stitched rosettes, or chunky twists of multi-stranded rope terminated with flouncy tassels or bulbous knots. Unlike the implied cool, smooth and hard texture of the plaster pieces, the fabric items appear silky, crinkled, delicate to the touch.

Arrange fabric borders at cornice level, looping them around the room, draped from floral rosettes, or make a dramatic feature of a single wall or chimney breast with a swagged arrangement that gives the impression of a drawn-back curtain around displays of real pictures or gilt-framed mirror. The pictures

The realms of fantasy brought to vivid life with paper cut-out, stick-on trompe l'oeil *architectural features, such as these convincing stone columns and balustrades in a mock neo-classical setting.*

themselves can be made to appear suspended on delicate twists of fabric topped with beautiful bows.

As with Baroque *trompe l'oeils*, a suitable background is important for achieving fabric effects. Plain colours on delicate paint-effect papers are the best choice, although it is permissible to hang an ordinary wallcovering with a pattern, so long as the design does not detract from the subtlety of the 'fabric' pieces. A narrow- or broad-striped paper, for example, is quite suitable, although a vivid floral pattern would only confuse the issue.

To illustrate the effectiveness of illusion, create a tented environment by hanging a real fabric or fabric-effect wallcovering such as a striped canvas; divide the ceiling diagonally to form four triangular segments and hang pieces of striped paper or fabric in each. Use thick rope *trompe l'oeils* vertically at each corner and diagonally across the ceiling, with 'knots' at the corner joints and tassels dangling from a rope frieze. Run lengths of rope along the floor and ceiling lines. At the centre of the ceiling hang an exotic chandelier or flounce of fabric created with stick-on pieces.

Paper swags and rosettes that resemble fabric used to frame or suspend real pictures or furniture, while linking the scheme with a continuous frieze at cornice level.

CHAPTER EIGHT

DIVIDING LINES

Broad, featureless walls can be boringly blank or oppressively dominant, but pre-cut printed strips and dado panels can be used to divide the space into manageable areas that can be decorated to create interest and restore comfortable proportion to a room.

Friezes and Borders

Patterned paper borders and embossed friezes can be used to divide walls, link decorative schemes throughout the house, frame interesting features or improve the proportions of the room. Many are sold to complement popular ranges of wallcovering.

Fashion during the late nineteenth-century dictated that walls should be divided into three areas – the dado at the bottom, a central filling, and a frieze below the ceiling – each of which is separated by moulded wooden rails. Each area was given a different decorative treatment, often with papers which were related in pattern or colour. Further emphasis was sometimes given to the divisions by applying painted or stencilled floral or classically geometric borders above or below the dado or picture rails.

Pre-cut and Pasted

Happily for today's home paperer, wallcovering manufacturers now produce ready-printed, often pre-pasted, borders and friezes to enhance their ranges. Most types of paper border can be stuck directly to a papered or painted wall (see the instructions on page 122 for further details). Embossed friezes are intended to simulate an ornate plaster cornice – featuring bold foliage or geometric patterns –and must be painted, perhaps in such a way that simulates time-worn patina. Many types are deep enough to fill the space between ceiling and picture rail. Because of their complexity, embossed friezes are only really suitable for hallways and elegant drawing rooms, rather than bedrooms where a more subtle border should be used.

A Sense of Proportion

Apart from their decorative function, friezes and borders can be used to good practical effect. In a tall room, for example, furniture will tend to be dwarfed unless it is large and upright; when seated, the walls will appear to loom over you.

The simple device of a horizontal frieze applied below the ceiling angle, running around the walls, will visually decrease the height of the room. An embossed frieze, painted a contrasting tone to the walls below will foreshorten the walls visually, while very high ceilings might benefit from being painted a rich colour, taken down onto the frieze, too.

Visual Link

Consider how you can use the device of a simple, narrow paper border to carry a decorative theme throughout the house, or create a neutral link for otherwise disparate areas. Starting in the entrance hall, as you enter the front door, fix the border at dado, skirting or cornice level (or at each level) where it will capture the focus of the eye and lead you up the stairway to the first floor landing and any passageway beyond.

Where a dado or skirting border encounters a doorway, you have the option of cutting it off at the edge of the architrave and picking it up at the other side of the opening, or else running the border up and over the architrave in a continuous band, then continuing it.

With a more intricately patterned or colourful border you can pick out elements of the design and use them as a basis for the decorative scheme within the rooms linked by the border: for example, taking a floral motif from the strip and using a paper with a larger version in a sitting room or bedroom.

Greater Emphasis

Emphasis can be given to a feature wall or focal point by running a paper border entirely around the perimeter, or set about 150 mm (6 in) away from the edge for greater impact: a dark-painted or -papered wall with a light perimeter band will dominate (the ideal backdrop for a display of beautiful paintings), while a paler-coloured wall with a vividly patterned margin will draw the attention without the risk of being overbearing (more suited to a wall containing a window overlooking an attractive view). Mitre the corners for neatness and continuity of pattern, or use one of the ready-made corner sections sold by some manufacturers: these sections commonly

Primrose yellow wallpaper with pale green cornflower foliage and blue buds is outlined with a cornflower blue border that frames each wall; the curtains match, but with cornflowers in bloom and blue piping.

incorporate ornate curves and bevels.

If you favour an overall plainer decorative scheme, with abstract detailing, use a textured paper such as woodchip or a subtly embossed Anaglypta for the main wall areas, painted cream or beige tone, then apply a narrow framing border, perhaps with a coordinating corner detail or flourish. Stepping the border angularly, say at the centre of the run of the wall, can produce an interesting focal point, below which you could hang an unframed picture with toning colouring.

Use this same framing technique to simulate the effect of smaller, three-dimensional panels on a wall, particularly a large, otherwise plain area. Rectangles or squares formed in neatly mitred paper borders can contain a large single picture or displays of several smaller frames, a fine gilt-framed mirror, or sections of a contrasting wallcovering with a decorative wall light as its centre.

Above: A pink ribbon-and-bow frieze runs around the room over a delicate vertical pink stripe wallpaper in this pretty cottage bedroom.

Right: Highly textured dado in tough lincrusta makes an ideal covering for a busy hallway.

Low Divisions

The dado combines a practical means of bearing the brunt of daily knocks with a decorative treatment that can lend the walls a more stately symmetry.

In early period properties a wainscot of matchboarding – narrow strips of tongue-and-grooved timber – was commonly applied to

HANGING DADO PANELS

Lincrusta dado panels come in two sizes, in cartons containing five panels plus top-edge border. The Art Nouveau panel size is 540 mm wide × 914 mm drop ($21\frac{1}{4}$ × 36 in); the Edwardian pattern measures 610 mm wide × 1016 mm drop (24 × 40 in). The pre-cut panels are straight-matching edge to edge, so there is no wastage with repeat patterns.

Special adhesive is needed to hang the panels on a cross-lined surface, after the backs have been soaked with warm water.

The dado panels can be decorated with an oil-based paint, in either gloss or semi-gloss finish, or can be 'distressed' with a scumble glaze to give an attractive patina of age.

the lower half of the walls in a vain attempt to conceal the effects of rising damp. No other provisions against damp existed, and the method actually promoted rot. This method of decoration, used extensively in hallways and dining rooms, was intended to protect the primitive plasterwork from abrasion by chair backs or the inevitable knocks from busy traffic (say, by prams), and eventually evolved into a simple moulded wooden 'chair' or 'dado' rail fixed horizontally about 900 mm (36 in) above floor level.

The dado – the area immediately below the rail – was popularly covered with a thick, durable embossed paper such as Anaglypta, and painted a rich, dark glossy colour. The thick, impervious nature of the dado no doubt helped to conceal the effects of rising damp, but did not offer a cure.

Imitative of ornate period plasterwork, this traditional style Empire frieze in durable textured Lincrusta has been decorated with a translucent scumble glaze to simulate the patina of age and accentuate its emboss.

Nowadays, although any tough embossed paper can be used below the dado rail, ready-trimmed panels are available for this precise purpose. Special dados in the Lincrusta range are still available today in their original Victorian and Edwardian designs. The former is a flowing art nouveau design featuring a stylized pear tree motif incorporating a linenfold border and broad, cross-hatched plinth; the other features a complex regular pattern of foliage on slender stems, with fluted bordering. Both types come with a roll of top-edge border formed in Lincrusta. Because the panels are pre-cut, there will be no wastage, except perhaps where the dado meets a doorway architrave.

Dado panels do not suit all styles of house, being more apt for town dwellings than for country residences or cottages. Nevertheless, these rustic settings often boasted original wooden wainscotting more in keeping with their Arts and Crafts atmosphere and generally smaller scale. In the true spirit of embossed papers as mimics of other materials, choose a design for your dado that accurately simulates timber: Lincrusta's waned oak pattern resembles open-grained overlapping planks, which can be scumble-glazed to give the appearance of stained wood. It comes on a roll and is intended for hanging horizontally. In similar vein there is a bamboo lattice design or, perhaps more authentic, a linenfold design simulating finely moulded timber panelling.

CHAPTER NINE

CUT AND STICK

Think of wallpaper in an entirely new way by using its printed motifs as a source of inspiration to co-ordinate a decorative scheme to furniture and furnishings, using the cut-and-stick process of découpage and collage.

Cut-out Motifs

Cut existing motifs, patterns or stripes of colour from excess or discontinued rolls of wallcovering and use them to adapt the design of another paper to create your own unique scheme.

Chopping up an expensive wallpaper is not usually considered by most people when decorating, but it is a technique which can be used to good effect – and an excellent way to use up any leftover paper from another room.

For all its flexibility in where and how you hang wallpaper, you are basically using someone else's creative prowess to decorate your home. The more experimental and artistic you are, the less you will be keen on plumping for the wallpaper designer's patterns *per se*. So learn to rethink how you approach the process of selecting wallcoverings from manufacturer's pattern books: consider how you can extract the elements of papers which appeal to you – the delicate shade that matches your upholstery, for example, a pretty flower, bird motif or geometric shape.

At its most basic, the idea can produce interesting effects. Take a broad striped wallpaper used as a dado in a long, narrow and tall hallway as an example; slice out one of the stripes in the more dominant colour, using a scalpel and long steel ruler. Paste the stripe and stick it along the top edge of the wooden dado rail to emphasize the break: continue the upper half of the wall in, say, a finer pinstripe paper of a similar colour.

Trim a second stripe from the wide-striped paper and stick it across the bottom of the dado along the top edge of the skirting. A further wide stripe cut from the paper can be applied at ceiling height as a token cornice. The finished effect gives good proportion to the high, narrow hallway. To continue the scheme up the staircase to the landing, trim a stripe from the paper and run it along the top edge of the staircase skirting.

Cut out geometric motifs (diamonds, stars or circles for example) or more free-form images (classical urns, Roman busts, cartoon characters) from an existing wallpaper, and stick these onto another plainer background paper to create your own wallpaper design (see page 87). It's essential to stick the cut-outs down well, so avoid curling and peeling.

A grey stripe cut from the grey and yellow dado paper is used to link the decorative scheme, and is run horizontally at skirting, top edge of the dado and frieze level.

Papering Doors and Furniture

Some of the first decorative papers were nothing more than printer's rejects used to decorate inside cupboards and chests. Expand the basic idea by papering sections of panelled doors, other interior joinery, and even items of furniture, to co-ordinate a room scheme.

Early householders are known to have used offcuts of patterned paper salvaged from publisher's rejects to decorate the insides of plain cupboards, and storage chests. It is a practice still relevant today, as little or no attention is commonly paid to these largely unseen dark

holes. It is a simple idea which can brighten up the interior of a poky closet or understairs cupboard, or create a link with the room in which it is located by using the same design, or a complementary design and colourway.

Left: Sections of wallpaper cut from a roll and stuck to the panels of a door create a unified scheme. Right: Cover the glass door panels of cabinets with fabric-look papers to soften the appearance and simulate a curtained window effect.

Practical, Pretty Linings

Freestanding cabinets with glazed doors can become display cases if the compartments behind the panes are papered to show off ornaments or books inside. If the cupboard is frequently used, it is advisable to use a tough vinyl or even an embossed paper, painted accordingly, to prevent wear.

Offcuts of paper make a cheap and simple form of drawer lining (a practice long used by

householders unwilling to waste perfectly good snippets). Simply held down with drawing pins pushed in at each corner, the paper will last indefinitely, provided that nothing scratches the surface. For this reason, reserve this treatment only for drawers that contain clothes, rather than items such as cutlery.

Decorating in Miniature

Use offcuts, too, in the decoration of a dolls' house, applying them to the walls with paste in just the same way as you would in your own rooms. Pattern choice is important for realism: obviously only the smallest, most delicate patterns are really suitable for the scaled-down surfaces of a dolls' house. Bear in mind the effects of colour, texture and pattern on the tiny rooms: the 'advancing' and 'receding' qualities apply in the same way as full-size rooms (see pages 22–24).

Papered Panels

Link panelled doors to an overall scheme by cutting sections of the main wallpaper and sticking them neatly and squarely in the recesses of the panels. Papers with small or medium-sized patterns are best, so you can avoid the motif being cut off unattractively at the edges.

Papering the panels of doors, cabinets and other furniture such as screens, and the insides of trunks, gives you the opportunity to experiment with *trompe l'oeil* effects. Pre-cut pieces, as described fully on pages 70–74, can be pasted and stuck on to create a clever illusion. Papered sections that purport to be colourful folds of fabric, or tasselled lengths of rope or braid that hang within an empty door panel can individualize your furniture and link it with the surrounding decor.

If your interior doors are plain flush types you can still create a panelled effect by fixing decorative wooden panel mouldings to the surface to simulate a true panelled effect. You can buy lengths of panel mouldings from timber merchants and D.I.Y. stores; mitre the corners of each length and pin onto the door face. Alternatively, obtain pre-formed moulding 'frames', which can be stuck to the surface of the door with peel-off adhesive backings. Paper the panels formed by the 'frames', as previously described.

A humid jungle hideaway created in a small, otherwise featureless bedroom by carrying the densely-patterned foliage paper over the ceiling, and across the panels of doors.

Découpage Decorations

Découpage, the process of decorating a surface with motifs or images cut from paper or card, is an excellent way to individualize items of furniture, doors and other joinery, using surplus wallpaper. Prepare the background by removing any polish or varnish by sanding, then apply a paint finish. When dry, stick on the cut-out pieces using wallpaper paste and allow to dry. Such small cut-outs will tend to curl at the edges, especially if they are stuck onto a door which is frequently used, so it's usual to coat the entire surface with successive coats of matt, gloss or semi-gloss varnish once the cut-outs are correctly positioned. After sufficient coats of varnish, the motifs will assume a distinctly three-dimensional appearance.

PAPERING A PANEL DOOR

Some preparation is necessary to prevent the paper simply peeling off the door panel. If the door is painted, remove the paint using a chemical paint stripper and scraper. Don't use a blow torch or hot air gun, however, as the heat may adversely affect the paint on the main part of the door. If the door is unpainted, but waxed, rub with wire wool soaked in white spirit to prepare the wood.

Cut the paper to size with a 12 mm ($\frac{1}{2}$ in)-wide border all round. Stick on the paper cut-out using a strong paste solution, allowing it to overlap the edge of the panel. Use a sharp scalpel to trim around the perimeter of the panel, and peel off the excess paper.

Collage Course

Pasted collage compositions of paper, cloth, photographs and miscellaneous items of interest can be juxtaposed as an intriguing, multi-textured and layered form of wall décor.

Create your own exciting wallcoverings with collaged fabric hangings or juxtaposed, layered paper offcuts, postcards, photographs and other memorabilia stuck directly to the surface of the walls. Obtain discontinued lines of wallpaper and use these as the basis of a wall collage, applying the paper as a main background effect, but tearing out sections and filling in with offcuts from other, contrasting rolls of wallpaper, or unrelated pieces of paper or fabric.

In this way it is possible to build up a fantastically detailed and intricately textured, overlaid picture, using other mediums such as personalized pieces of paper, letters received from friends or relations, selections of your child's early paintings, holiday snapshots, colourful present wrappers, newspapers, or telephone doodles torn from your notepad. The source of collage materials is endless.

Theme your collage for continuity – musical scores, pictures of musicians, instruments, for example in a cacophony of suggested sound – or opt for a totally abstract, random effect. But whichever you choose, be sure to concentrate on the basic rules for colour, texture and pattern in order to avoid a mish-mash that will only resemble the contents of a wastepaper basket.

Embellish a flimsy fabric drape with dyed symbols or lettering, pieces of brown wrapping paper, tin foil or tissue stuck, sewn or pinned on, and suspend the hanging from a slim dowel curtain pole attached to the wall

Paper collage wall hangings suspended from a pole make a dramatic alternative to ordinary paper, illustrated with various motifs such as photographs, scribbled notes and pieces of fabric.

with brackets. Alternatively, stick the fabric wallcovering, allowing inevitable creases to add to the texture of the collage.

Confining the collage to a fairly small area is best, as too much texture and fine detail can be oppressive: create a collaged panel rather like a framed picture, surrounded by timber panel mouldings fixed to the wall, or use the collaged effect below a dado rail. If all the pieces that make up the collage are well stuck-down you can apply successive coats of matt, gloss or satin finish varnish as a surface seal, enabling you to wash the design when grubby.

As well as using collages as wall décor you can also apply them to items of furniture. For instance, make use of surplus wallpaper used conventionally throughout a room to link furniture such as a screen, chair, table or ornaments in a zany co-ordinated scheme.

Classical script, musical notation and other writings painted or stencilled onto fabric or paper wall hangings create a fascinating decorative feature, here linked to an antique chair re-upholstered to blend for unity.

CHAPTER TEN

PUTTING THEORY INTO PRACTICE

Having the inspiration to create lavish, unique decorative treatments with wallcoverings is only half the battle – for unless you know the correct method for hanging the various papers, vinyls and fabrics your beautiful vision is likely to become an eyesore. Here is a comprehensive instructional guide to making your decorative designs a reality.

After soaking, paste is applied to the back of a Lincrusta dado panel, using a paintbrush. The paste must be spread quite thickly for full coverage so that the panel will stick firmly.

Tools and Equipment

Even the simplest wallpapering job requires some specialist tools, so don't be tempted to improvize or the results will be second-rate. All the tools are readily available from do-it-yourself stores and decorator's merchants. Assemble a comprehensive armoury of tools and equipment so you can tackle the job with confidence, using this checklist as a guide:

Preparation

- **Scrapers** A stiff, wide, metal blade in a plastic or wooden handle, used to strip old wallcoverings and loose paint during preparation. Modern proprietary scrapers have replaceable blades, and incorporate a roller. The blade must be held at the correct angle to the wall to prevent gouging the plasterwork.
- **Steam stripper** Proprietary steam strippers are rather like large domestic irons: the integral tank is filled with water and the tool plugged into the mains. Steam is ejected from the sole of the plate to soften and loosen the old paste and paper. Used in conjunction with a scraper. Hired versions are normally bulky and unwieldy.
- **Sanding block and abrasives** After filling cracks and holes in walls or ceilings, use fine-grade abrasive paper wrapped around a wooden or plastic sanding block to give a smooth surface. Abrasive-coated sponge blocks are used in the same way, but must be rinsed in water periodically to prevent clogging.

Access Equipment

- **Stepladders** Normally straight drops can be hung from a pair of stepladders; you can create a walkway for reaching ceilings with two stepladders and a scaffold board between the rungs. A multi-purpose stepladder is a good choice as it can be folded into numerous formats to cope with stairways, or to give a platform for reaching ceiling height.
- **Extending ladders** To reach high stairwell walls, an extending ladder is invaluable. Pad the ends of the stiles with cloths to protect the walls from scratches.
- **Decorator's trestles** For large walls or ceilings a set of decorator's trestles can be hired. The set-up comprises metal scaffold sections which slot together and support walking boards.

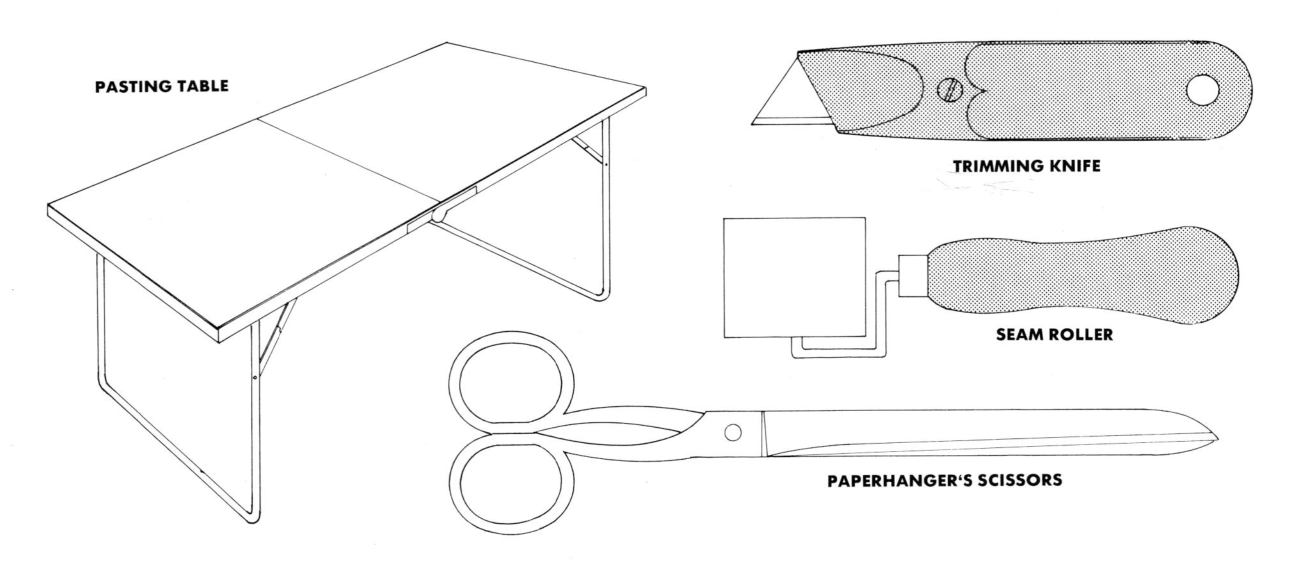

Papering

- **Pasting table** Although you can make do with any table with a wipe-clean surface, you will find that an inexpensive folding, purpose-made pasting table is easist to move around to keep close to the work. The top can be kept at just the right height.
- **Pasting brush** A proprietary pasting brush is better than an ordinary paintbrush, as the bristles are coarser and stiffer, and the brush itself is broader, allowing you to spread on the paste evenly. Some pasting brushes have a hook which enables you to clip the brush onto the rim of the paste bucket when not in use.
- **Bucket or bowl** A plastic bucket or bowl is used for mixing and containing the paste. Tie a piece of string across the rim of the bucket and use to scrape off excess paste from the bristles of the pasting brush.
- **Roller** With some wallcoverings you have to paste the wall and a roller is by far the easiest method. Use a short pile or foam roller in conjunction with an ordinary paint tray for loading the roller.
- **Paperhanger's brush** Use for smoothing the paper onto the wall and pushing folds into corners, there is no real substitute for a special paperhanger's brush. The bristles are normally held within a wooden handle.
- **Soft roller** Felt and rubber rollers are needed for smoothing fabrics, metal foil and veneer wallcoverings.
- **Sponge** A synthetic sponge is often useful for smoothing on pre-pasted wallcoverings and vinyls, and used damp for wiping off smears from the face of the wallcovering.
- **Seam roller** A hard plastic or wooden roller about 25 mm (1 in) wide, used to flatten butt-joins between lengths of paper or vinyl.
- **Trimming knife** A replaceable-blade knife, preferably with a curved cutting edge, is used for trimming wallcoverings.
- **Straight-edge** A metal straight-edge, such as a steel rule, is used in conjunction with the trimming knife for cutting straight lines, such as through overlapping layers to produce a butt-join.
- **Tape measure** A retractable steel tape measure is essential for measuring lengths or widths of wallcovering.
- **Pencil** Use for marking wallcoverings for cutting, and for creasing paper into ceiling/wall angles prior to trimming.
- **Scissors** Paperhanging scissors have long blades designed to cut easily through various wallcoverings; the outer edge of the blade is shaped for creasing paper into corners.
- **Plumbline and bob** A string with a weight (bob) on the end, which is used to mark vertical lines on a wall: by chalking the stringline, a guideline can be marked on the wall by twanging the string against the surface. Choose a bob that is flat so that it can hang as close to the wall as possible without touching for more accurate positioning.

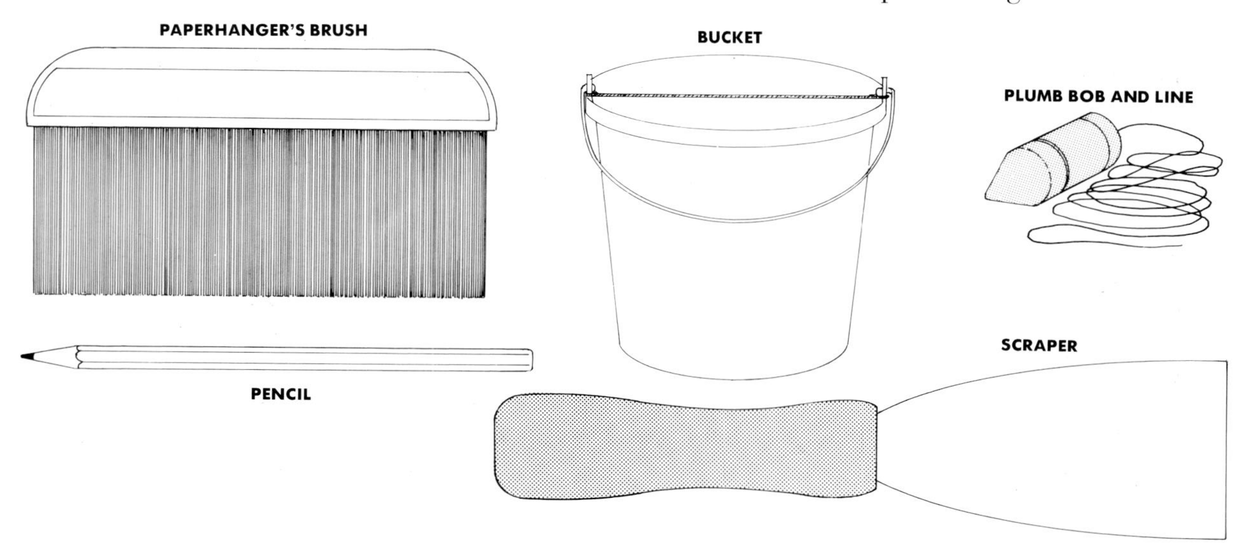

Surface Preparation

Although many wallcoverings – say, whites such as woodchip – will conceal hairline cracks and minor surface imperfections, others, notably foils, will actually highlight defects. Thorough preparation of the walls (and ceiling) is therefore essential.

Wash down grubby or dusty surfaces with a proprietary sugar soap solution, then rinse with clean water and allow to dry. Check that the plasterwork is fairly sound, reasonably dry and flat. Rake out cracks wider than about 6 mm ($\frac{1}{4}$ in) with a knife, fill using premixed fine-surface filler, then sand smooth. Remake chipped external corners with stiff general-purpose filler applied with a filling knife, and run fine-surface filler down cracks in internal corners with a rubber-gloved finger.

Not all previously hung wallcoverings are suitable for over-hanging with new coverings, so it's best to strip them off. Ordinary papers – plus the old adhesive – can be softened prior to scraping by soaking with a proprietary stripping powder mixed with warm water and applied with a houseplant sprayer. Washables and papers that have been painted with gloss must be scored with a serrated scraper so that the stripper can penetrate. Vinyls can usually be stripped by peeling off the top film from the bottom corner, leaving the backing paper in place as a lining; fabrics and foils can be peeled off similarly. To remove stubborn wallcoverings use a steam stripper. Avoid bulky hired types: electric versions, rather like a domestic iron, are lightweight and easy to use.

Walls to be repapered – especially if the plasterwork is powdery or porous – should be sized to improve slip during hanging and prevent too much paste being absorbed before the paper sticks. Sizing involves painting on a liberal coat of diluted wallpaper adhesive and allowing it to dry.

Ceilings are susceptible to cracking caused by the flexing of the floor above, while nicotine from cigarettes, grease from the cooker and leaky pipes are often responsible for stains. Wash off grime with sugar soap, applied with a long-handled squeegee mop. Seal stubborn stains such as nicotine with aluminium sealer paint or a proprietary spray-on stain sealer. Previous coats of distemper on a ceiling would prevent paper from sticking, so it must be laboriously removed by sponging and scraping.

Neither plasterboard ceilings nor walls will endure extensive wet-stripping, unless the surface was previously sealed, so dry-stripping is the only option. Take care not to gouge the surface.

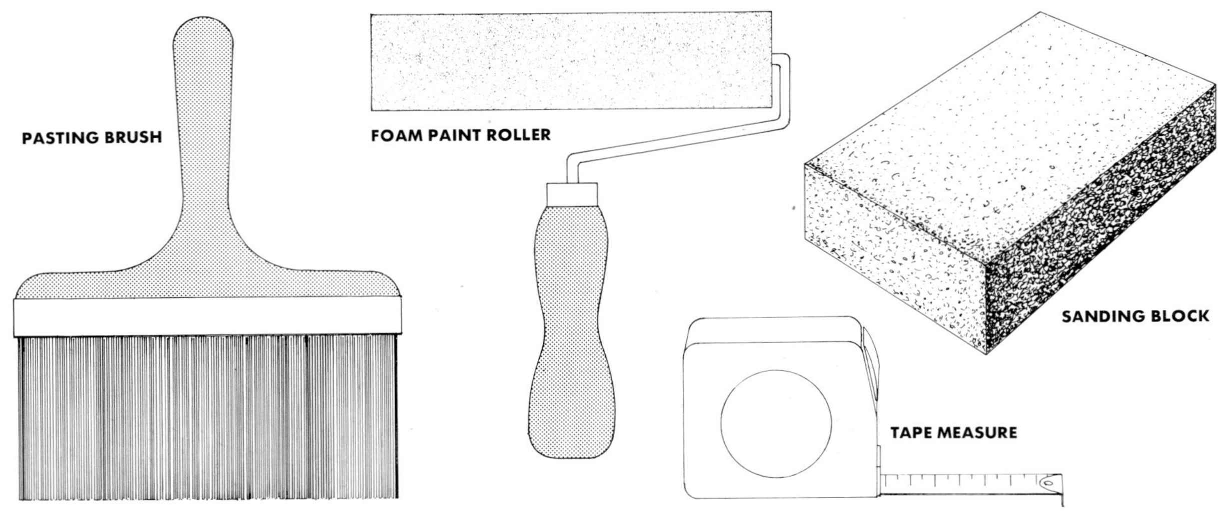

Stripping Wallcoverings

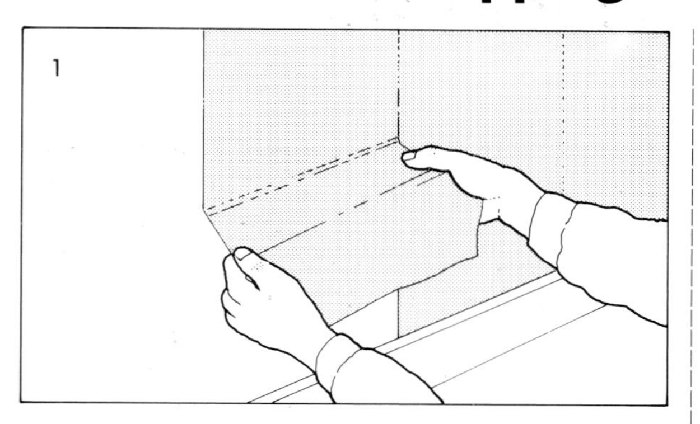

Peel away the top layer of a vinyl wallcovering from a bottom corner and strip off the top film, leaving the paper backing in place as lining paper.

Jets in the baseplate of a steam stripper force steam into the wallcovering, softening it and the adhesive. Scrape off the sodden paper with a knife.

Filling Cracks

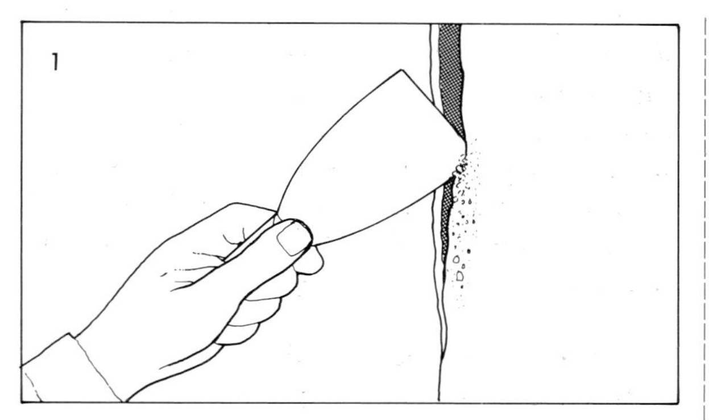

Rake out loose material from cracks using a scraping knife and undercut the edges so the filler material will grip. Brush out debris with an old paintbrush.

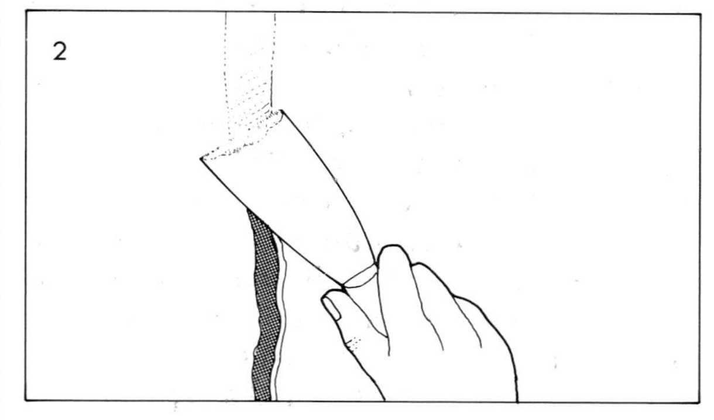

Dampen the crack with clean water then spread premixed filler along it with a filling knife, pressing it well into the undercut edges.

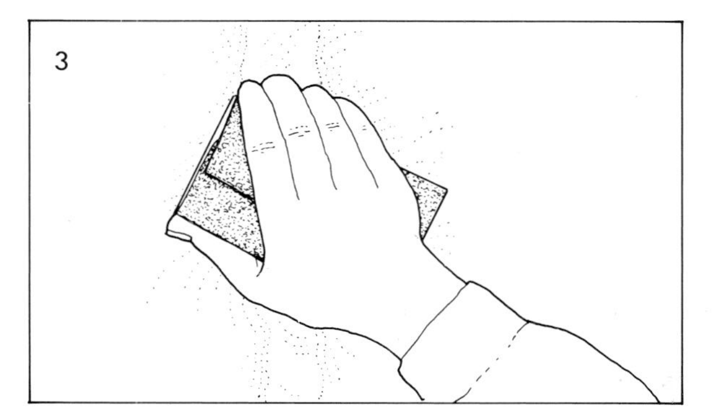

When the filler has hardened, rub down the patch with fine-grade glasspaper wrapped around a wood block so it is flush with the surrounding wall surface.

Repairing Chipped Corners

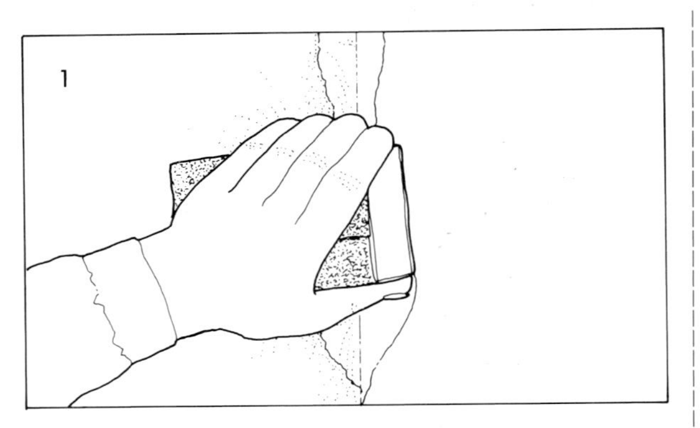

Spread stiff filler onto both sides of a chipped corner using a filling knife, working from the corner. When hard, sand smooth both sides of the angle.

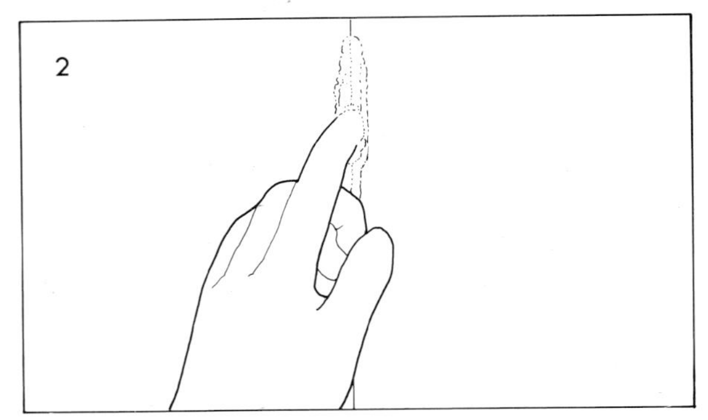

Fill a crack in an internal corner by dipping a rubber-gloved finger into filler and running it along the defect. When set, smooth with a fold of abrasive paper.

Estimating Wallcoverings

A standard roll measures 10.5 m (11 yd) long × 530 mm (21 in) wide, although specials might be wider, narrower, longer or shorter. For a standard roll, measure the room from the top of the skirting to the ceiling and around the walls then consult the chart below to determine how many rolls you will need.

For non-standard wallcoverings, measure the height of the room, adding 100 mm (4 in) for trimming, then divide this length into the length of a roll to give the number of strips you can cut from a roll. Use a length of string to plot widths of paper around the room then divide this number by the number of strips from one roll to give the number of rolls you will need. It's best to overestimate for wastage, and where pattern repeats are large, by ordering an extra roll.

Walls		Measurement around walls including doors and windows												
Height from skirting		Metres												
		9.1	10.4	11.6	12.8	14.0	15.2	6.5	17.7	18.9	20.1	21.3	22.6	23.8
		Feet												
		30	34	38	42	46	50	54	58	62	66	70	74	78
Metres	Feet													
2.15–2.30	7–7½	4	5	5	6	6	7	7	8	8	9	10	10	10
2.30–2.45	7½–8	5	5	6	6	7	7	8	8	9	9	10	11	11
2.45–2.60	8–8½	5	5	6	7	7	8	9	9	10	10	12	12	12
2.60–2.75	8½–9	5	5	6	7	7	8	9	9	10	10	12	12	12
2.75–2.90	9–9½	6	6	7	7	8	9	9	10	10	11	12	13	13
2.90–3.05	9½–10	6	6	7	8	8	9	10	10	11	12	13	14	14
3.05–3.20	10–10½	6	7	8	8	9	10	10	11	12	13	14	15	15
		Number of rolls required												
Number of rolls for ceilings		2	2	2	3	3	4	4	4	5	5	6	7	7

Cutting and Pasting

Organize yourself prior to hanging wallcovering by measuring the height of the walls and cutting the paper to length. Allow about 50 mm (2 in) for trimming and pattern matching top and bottom. It's useful to mark off the top of your pasting table in 300 mm (12 in) increments and use this as a rule for measuring 'drops' of paper. With several drops cut, you will be able to establish a working rhythm: while one is being hung another is pasted and soaking.

Accurate pattern-matching is vital for the appearance of the wallcovering – and to save on wastage. Lay the first drop on the pasting table, pattern uppermost and unroll another length on top. Align the pattern and cut the second strip, remembering to allow excess for trimming top and bottom. Bear in mind the pattern of the particular wallcovering you are using: on some 'drop pattern' papers the pattern runs diagonally and you will have to start the second length half a pattern repeat further along. Lay several drops face down on the pasting table, preventing them from curling with string looped around the table legs.

Cellulose-based paste, sold as powder or flakes, is used for standard wallcoverings: mix with water as instructed. Ordinary and heavy-duty pastes are available for medium- and heavy-weight papers respectively, although all-purpose types will suit both, usually with less water added for heavy papers. A fungicidal paste is best for vinyls and washables so mould will not form behind them.

The paste must be allowed to soak in so that the paper will expand to its limit – this can be up to 1.2 mm ($\frac{1}{2}$ in) in length; 25 mm (1 in) in width – or it will stretch while on the wall and cause bubbles. Medium-weight papers require about five minutes soaking time but heavy-weights must be left for up to 15 minutes. Ready-pasted papers must be thoroughly soaked in a special tray prior to hanging, to activate the adhesive. Paste three drops of medium-weight paper so that the first is ready for hanging by the time you have pasted and folded the third; prepare six drops of heavy-weight paper.

Apply the paste with a broad pasting brush, first down the centre, then to each side. Slide the paper so it overhangs the edge of the table when brushing outwards to avoid smearing the face of the wallcovering with paste. Fold the pasted paper onto itself in a large overlap, but do not press down or it will stick. Slide the drop along the table and complete the pasting, then fold over a smaller overlap. Drape the folded paper over a broom handle between two chair backs and leave to soak for the recommended period.

It was traditional practice to start papering from the window and around the room away from the light so that overlaps would be in shadow, but with the modern technique of butt-jointing papers this is not necessary: start hanging the paper in a corner behind the main door, where pattern loss will not be noticeable. Alternatively, hang the first length centrally on a chimney breast and work outwards from each side.

Measuring and Cutting

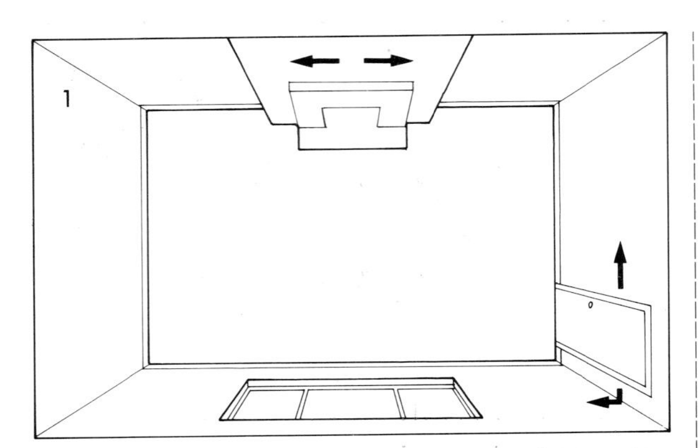

Start papering in the corner near the door so that any loss of pattern will be least noticeable, or begin at the centre of a chimney breast for symmetry.

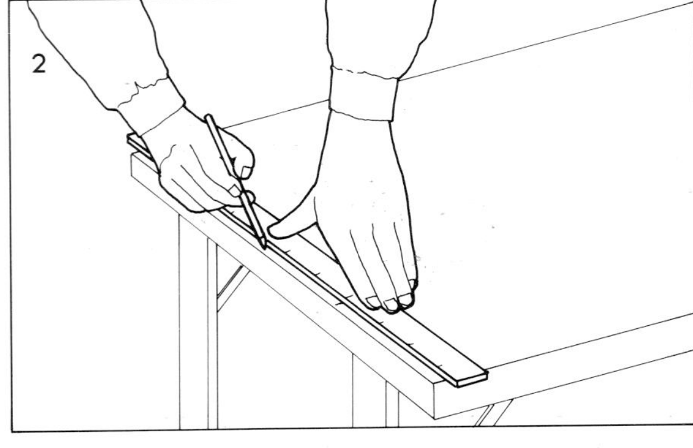

It is useful to mark off the top long edge of the pasting table in increments of 300 mm (12 in) to use as a handy means of measuring drops straight from the roll.

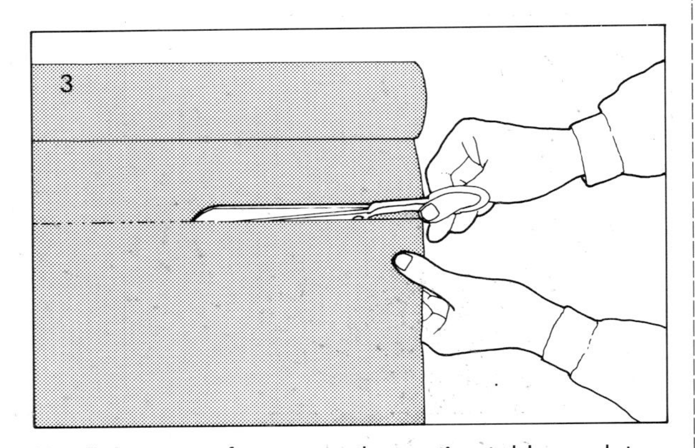

Unroll the paper face-up on the pasting table, mark to length according to the makeshift measure, then trim squarely using a pair of long-bladed scissors.

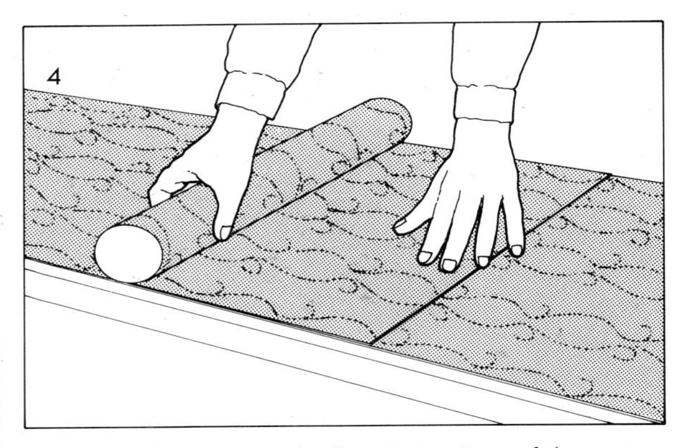

If the paper is patterned, align the pattern of the first, unroll, then cut to size, allowing extra paper for trimming.

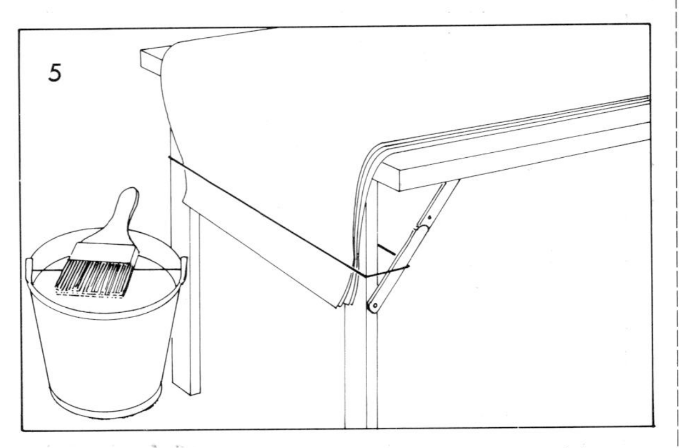

Lay several lengths face-down on the pasting table held by string loops. String tied across the rim of the paste bucket is used to wipe surplus paste from the brush.

USING READY-PASTED WALLCOVERINGS

Ready-pasted wallcoverings are rolled face inwards and soaked in a special water trough. After the specified amount of time, pull the top out and place directly on the wall.

Pasting the Paper

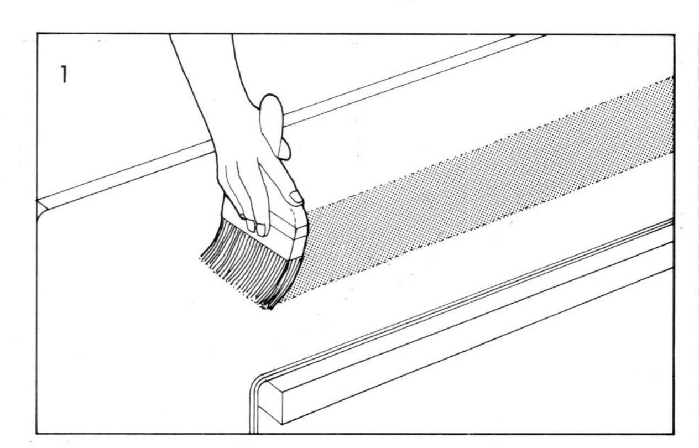

Load the brush generously with paste and, standing facing the light so you can see unpasted areas, brush along the centre of the paper.

Slide the top length of paper so it overhangs the far edge of the pasting table and brush the paste from the centre away from you along its length.

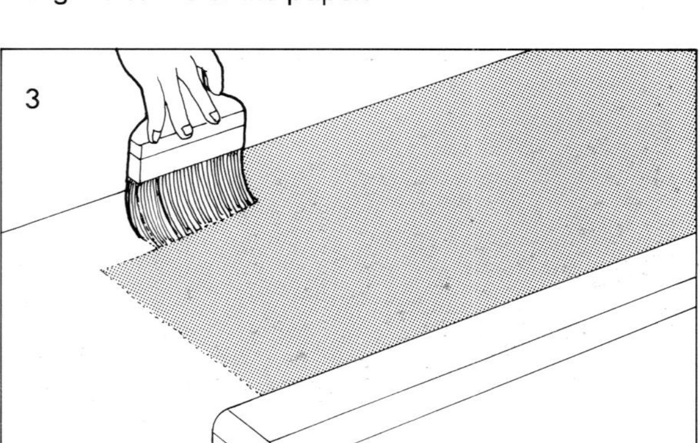

Slide the paper so it overhangs the near edge of the table. Brush out the paste towards you. Take care not to over-brush the paste or it may start to coagulate.

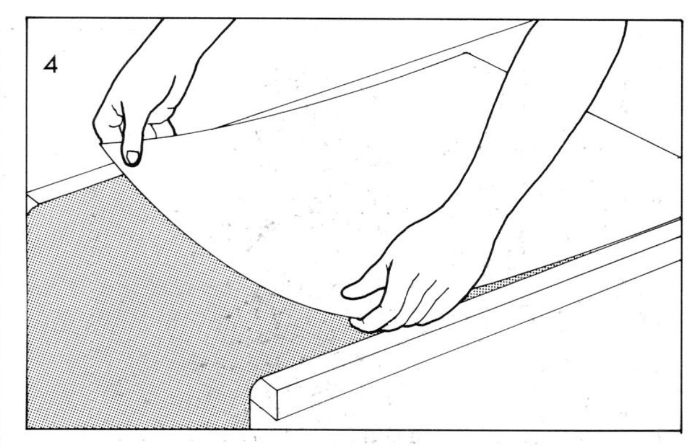

Fold the pasted length of paper onto itself but do not press down or it will stick. Slide the length of paper along the table and paste the remaining section.

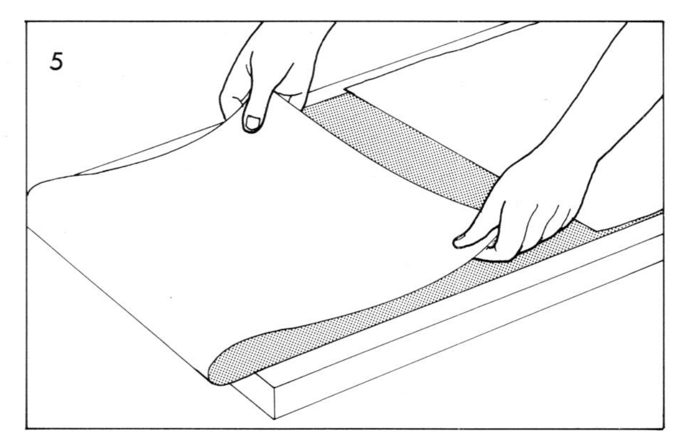

Fold the shorter length of pasted paper onto itself without pressing down or causing creases. This shorter fold tells you that this is the bottom of the drop.

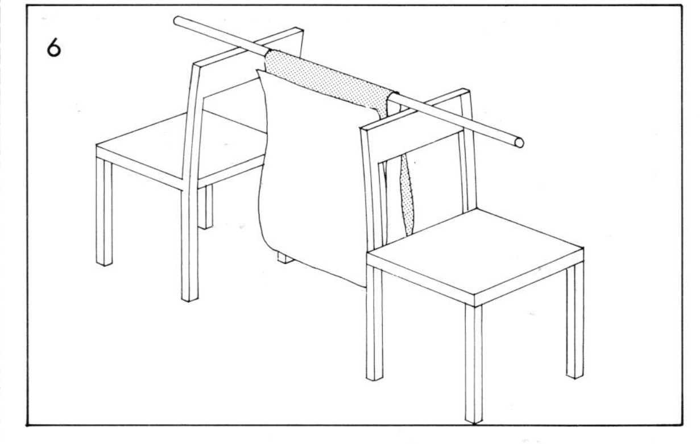

Suspend the pasted, folded length of wallcovering over a broom handle between the backs of a pair of chairs and leave to soak for the specified time.

Hanging Lining Paper

Buff-coloured lining paper is used to provide a neutral background of even porosity for the better quality wallcoverings and unbacked fabrics, and can be used to give a fairly flat finish to a previously patched surface. You must not, however, use it to strengthen badly cracked or crumbly plasterwork. Lining paper is hung in a similar way to ordinary wallpaper, except that it is fixed horizontally so that no butt-joins between strips will align with butt-joins between the lengths of wallcovering.

There are numerous thicknesses and densities of lining paper available to suit the condition of the wall and the covering you are applying. In general, you should choose a thicker paper for rough walls and heavy-weight wallcoverings, and thinner ones for fairly even walls and light- to medium-weight coverings. When used in conjunction with an open-weave fabric, such as hessian, the lining paper can be painted the colour of the wall-covering for a subtle effect, or a contrasting colour for a more vivid effect.

Lining paper is also used to give an even base for decorating directly with paint. Drops are hung vertically, with butt-joins between each, which become virtually invisible when painted.

Any indents remaining after lining paper has been hung can be made good with fine-surface filler and sanded smooth with fine abrasive paper. Before hanging the wallcovering over lining paper, make sure it is properly stuck down and the surface thoroughly dry to avoid loss of adhesion.

To hang the paper, first measure down from the ceiling in roll-width increments and draw horizontal lines around the walls at this point, using a pencil, spirit level and long batten of wood as a ruler. Cut long strips of lining paper to length, paste and fold concertina-fashion. Allow them to soak for just a few minutes then start hanging horizontally at the top of the wall.

Cross-lining

Start hanging the lining paper horizontally at the top of the wall, without overlapping the ceiling. Smooth it into place with a paperhanger's brush.

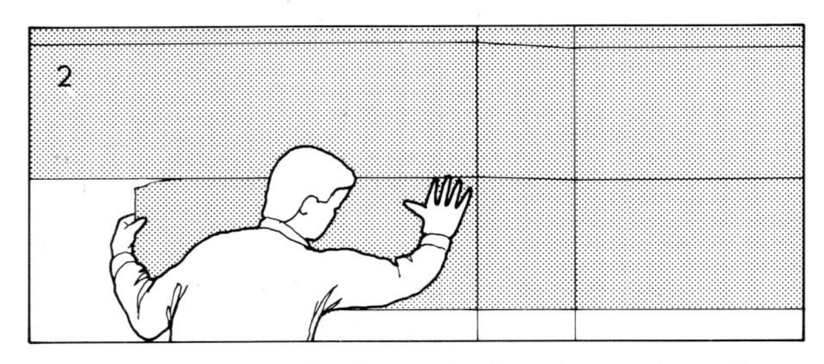

Hang the second and subsequent lengths, working down the wall. If the walls are fairly square you can turn the paper around corners.

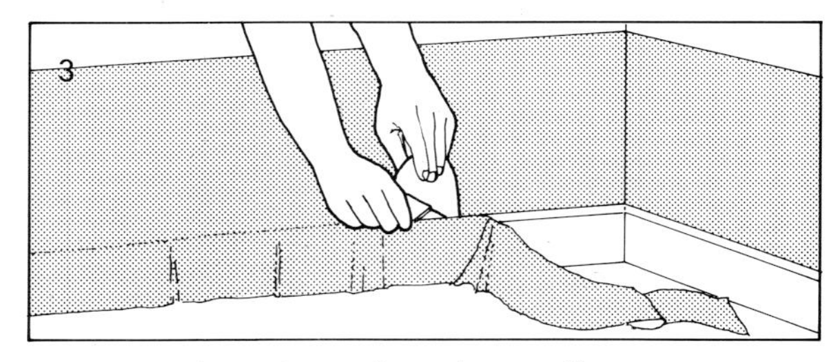

At the top of the skirting board, trim off any excess lining paper by running a sharp trimming knife along the top edge against a scraper.

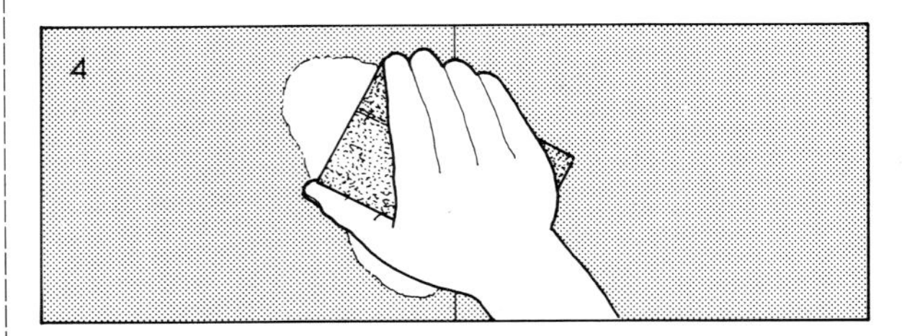

Any indents still remaining after lining a wall can be filled with fine-surface cellulose filler then, when set, sanded smooth.

Basic Papering

Most wallcoverings are hung vertically with their long edges butt-joined. Even though the joins will be inconspicuous, it's essential that each drop is hung vertically so that any pattern will not be misaligned. The ideal starting point for hanging wallcoverings is in a corner behind the room door, where any loss of pattern will not be noticeable. You cannot rely on the walls being straight, so mark guidelines to which you can match the wallcovering.

Use a roll to work out the positions of the widths of paper: if you find that there will be a very narrow strip at the end of the run, lessen the width of the first drop to give a wider strip at the end. Measure the width of the first strip from the starting corner and use a plumbline to mark a vertical pencil line at this point. Pin the plumbline to the top of the wall and allow the weighted end to swing until it stops at vertical. Mark the wall against the string.

Remove any cupboards or other fixtures where possible prior to pasting to avoid complicated cuts. Matchsticks pushed into the wallplugs left in the wall will pierce the wallcovering when it is hung, indicating positions for refixing the units or fittings.

Cut, paste and fold the first length of paper and allow to soak. When ready, drape over one arm and carry to the wall for hanging. A pair of stepladders should suffice for reaching the top of the wall: climb up and unfold the larger fold of the paper and press against the wall. Slide the top of the strip to align its edge with the pencil line and allow the paper to overlap onto the return wall and the ceiling.

Brush the paper upwards and outwards using a paperhanger's brush, then slowly descend the steps until you are able to unfold the smaller fold. Brush the paper onto the wall down to the skirting.

Run a pencil along the ceiling overlap – don't use the blade of your scissors; they give a thick, inaccurate line – then peel the paper away and trim off the overlap with long-bladed scissors. Brush the paper back onto the wall. Repeat for the skirting overlap. If you have prepared beforehand, the second drop of paper should be ready to hang straight away: brush it onto the wall, butting its edge up to the first drop. Run a wooden or plastic seam roller along the butt-joins of ordinary (non-embossed) wallcoverings to ensure that the edges are properly stuck down. Paste unstuck edges using a fine artist's paintbrush.

Ready-pasted paper is hung similarly, except that the drop is rolled up face innermost and placed in a trough of water positioned immediately below its place on the wall: by pulling the end of the paper out of the trough, you can brush it directly onto the wall, then use a sponge to wipe off excess water.

To paper around obstructions such as electrical socket outlets and light switches, hang the paper in the normal way then press gently onto the faceplate to form an indent. Peel back the paper to this point and pierce at the centre of the indent. Make diagonal cuts to each corner of the indent then press the paper back against the wall. Crease each flap of paper against the edge of the faceplate, then trim off with a sharp scalpel. For a neater finish (with any wallcovering except metal foil types), turn off the electricity at the main switch, loosen the screws holding the faceplate and draw it forward. Cut each flap a fraction too long then tuck the edges behind the faceplate. Replace the faceplate and restore the power.

To paper behind a radiator, paste a full length of paper only about half way down and hang as far as this from the top. Feed the paper behind the radiator as far as the brackets, crease it then pull out again. Cut from the bottom of the paper as far as each crease, then make diagonal cuts to each corner. Hold the bottom of the paper up the wall and apply the paste; wait for a few minutes, then smooth the paper down behind the radiator, using a long-handled paint roller.

Hanging Straight Drops

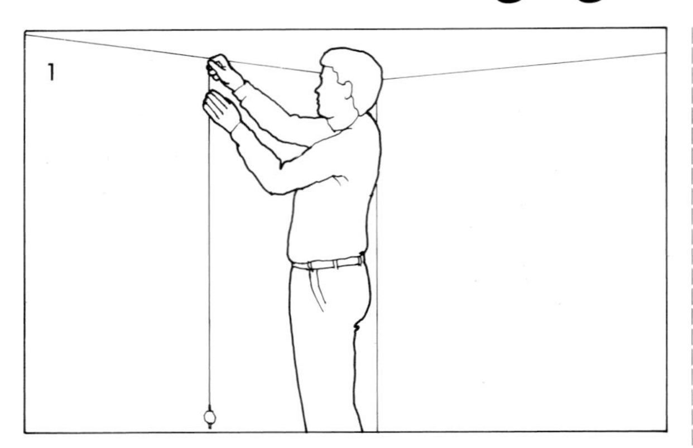

Work out the spacing of the rolls then use a plumbline to draw a vertical guideline against which you can hang the first drop.

Carry the pasted, folded paper over one arm to avoid creasing it, with the large fold facing you. Climb the stepladder, placed close to the wall.

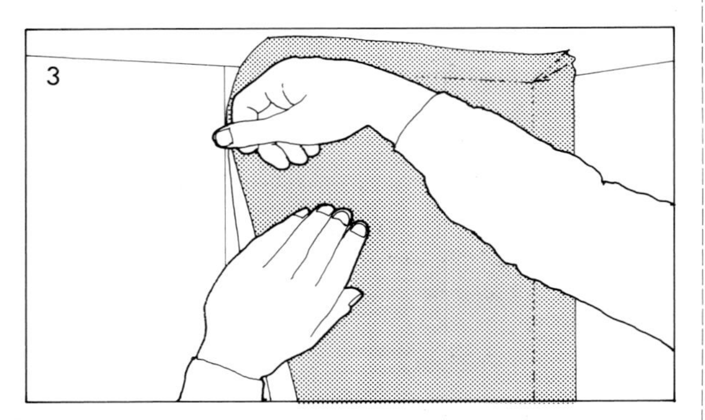

Unpeel the large fold of paper and press against the wall. Allow overlaps at ceiling and return wall; align the outer edge with the plumbed line.

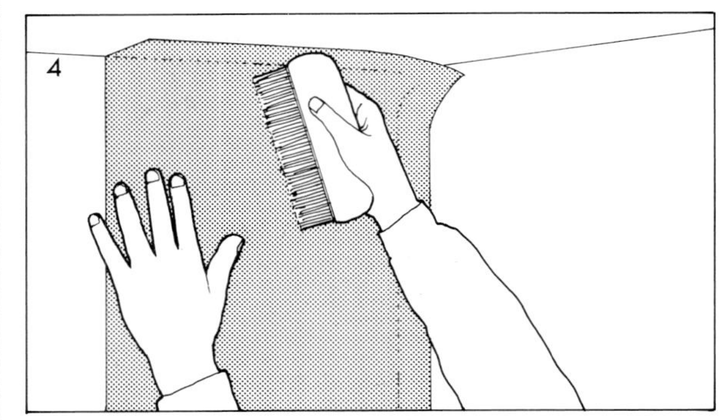

Brush the paper onto the wall, with upward and outward strokes, avoiding creases and bubbles by peeling back above them then brushing flat again.

Climb down the stepladder and unpeel the smaller bottom fold, then brush downward and outward alternately as far as the skirting board.

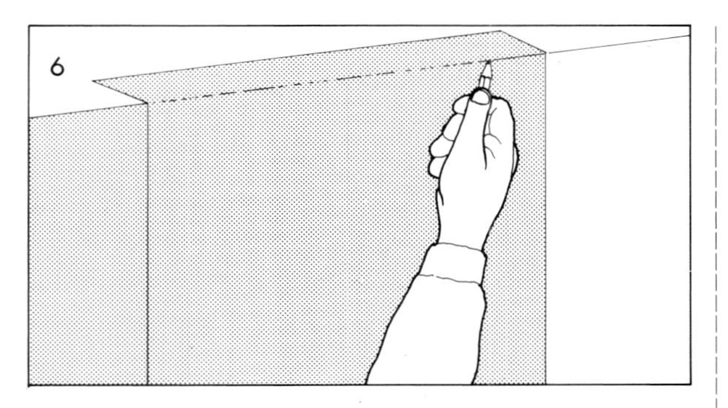

Scribe a pencil line along the ceiling and skirting angle to indicate the amount to be trimmed off. Wet paper tears easily so don't press too hard.

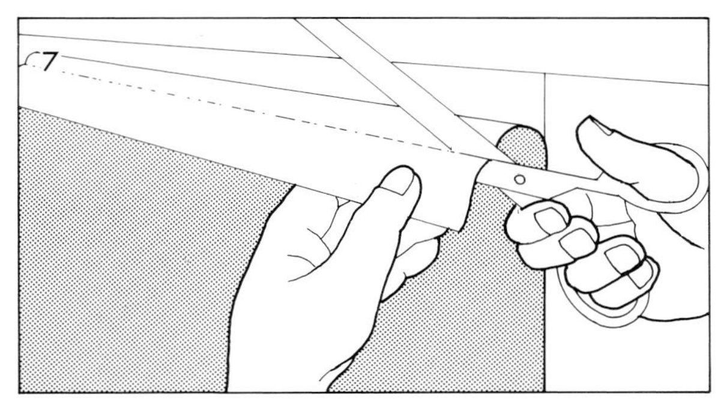

Peel away the paper at the top and cut off the overlap using long-bladed scissors. Brush the paper back onto the wall. Repeat for the skirting angle.

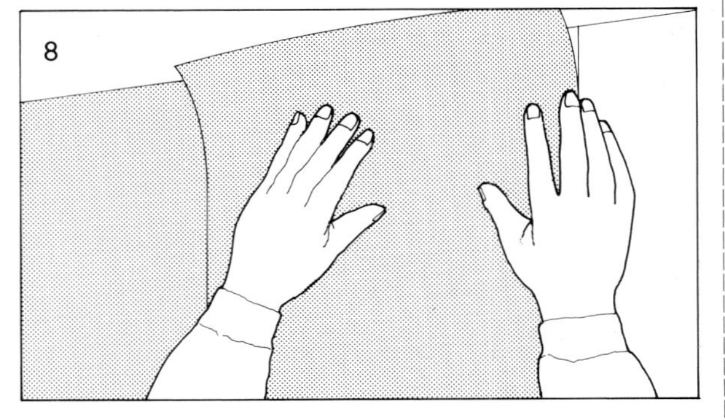

Place the second drop of paper against the wall, its edge butted up to that of the first drop. Brush flat and trim at top and bottom as before.

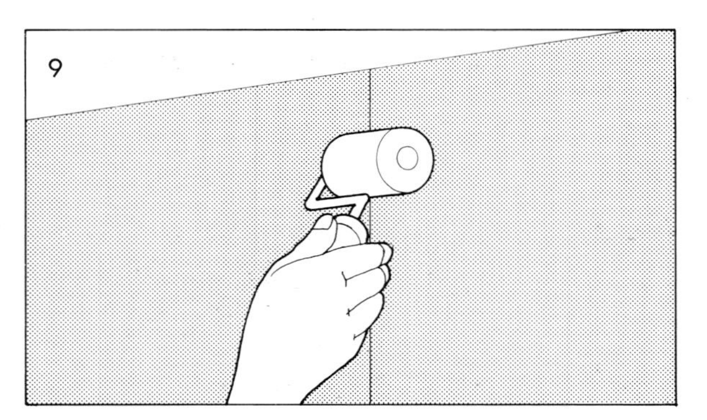

Run a seam roller along the butt join to make sure the edges stick. Use fresh paste on an artist's paintbrush to touch in unstuck areas.

Papering Around Obstructions

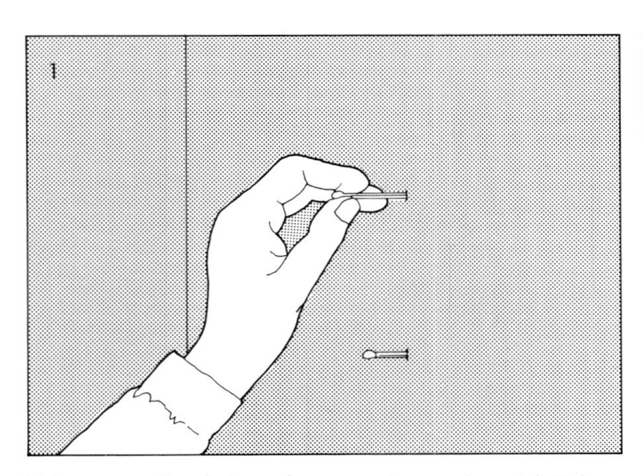

When removing fixtures for papering, push matchsticks into the wallplugs so they will pierce the paper to indicate fixing points.

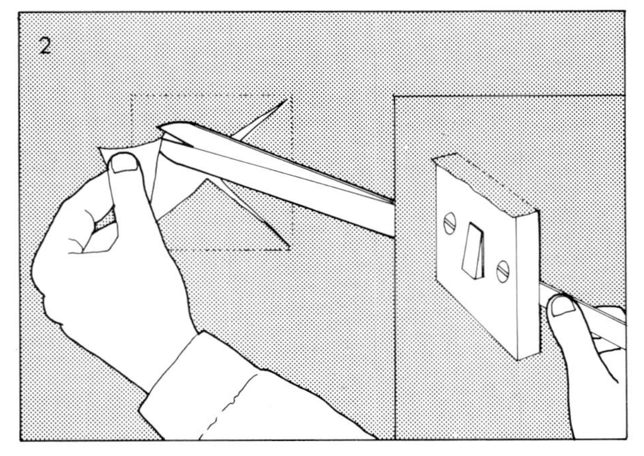

Press the paper against a switch or socket to form an indent; cut into the corners. Trim the flaps and tuck behind the fitting faceplate.

(Continued on page 104)

Papering Behind Radiators

Paste and hang half a drop and crease against the radiator brackets. Cut from the bottom to each crease; make diagonal cuts the width of the brackets.

Hold the bottom of the length up the wall and paste. When it has soaked, feed behind the radiator and press against the wall using a radiator roller.

Papering Around Corners

It is unlikely that the corners of a room will be truly square – especially in older houses – and any wallpaper turned around them will probably crease. Although small overlaps are permissible at corners, they should be avoided elsewhere. However, corners can be dealt with in a neat and effective way by using the following method.

On an internal corner, measure the distance between the last-hung drop and the corner at the top, centre and bottom, and add 6 mm ($\frac{1}{4}$ in) to the widest dimension to give an adequate overlap. Trim a narrow strip to this width, paste and fold the paper, then leave to soak. Hang the paper in the gap between the last whole drop and the corner, brushing the overlap onto the return wall.

To continue papering on the return wall, measure out from the corner the width of the offcut plus 6 mm ($\frac{1}{4}$ in) and drop a plumbline at this point. Paste and hang the offcut so that the outer edge is aligned with the guideline and the inner edge covers the small overlap from the return wall. Expect some loss of pattern at the corner.

To tackle an external corner, turn the paper about 25 mm (1 in) onto the return wall and tear the overlap to create a 'feathered', thinner edge and avoid a harsh line showing through. Drop a plumbline on the return side of the corner, a full roll width away from the corner plus an allowance of 6 mm ($\frac{1}{4}$ in), then paste and hang a length of wallpaper so that it covers the overlap but is set back from the corner by the extra allowance.

Remember when overlapping wallpaper that vinyl types will not stick to themselves. Always use latex adhesive instead of ordinary paste at corners, then flatten the overlap using a seam roller.

Papering Internal Corners

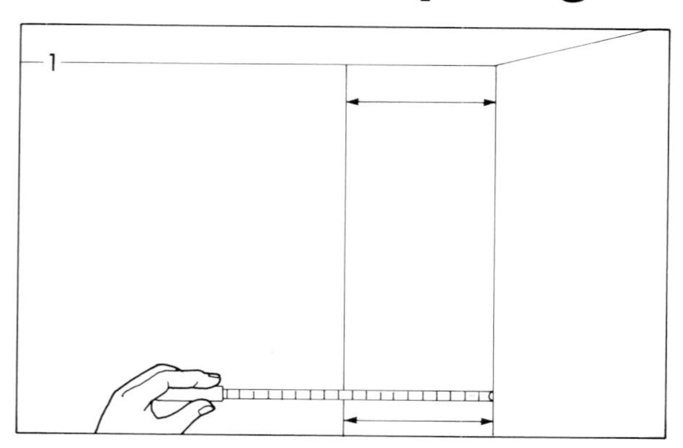

Measure from the last-hung full-width drop into the corner at top, centre and bottom to determine the width of offcut needed.

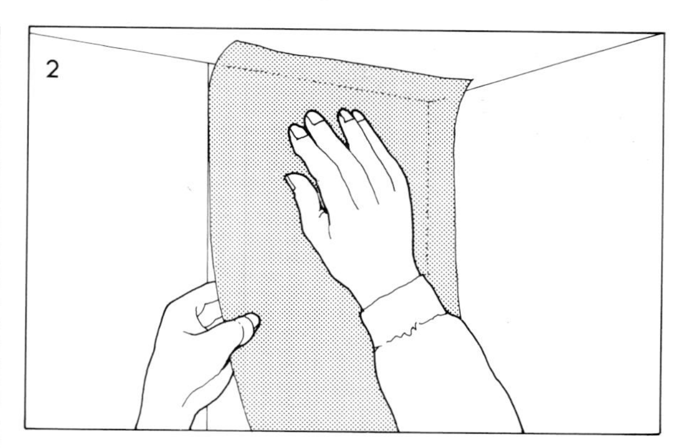

Add 6 mm ($\frac{1}{4}$ in) to the widest dimension and cut a strip of wallpaper to this width. Paste the paper, allow to soak, then brush into the corner.

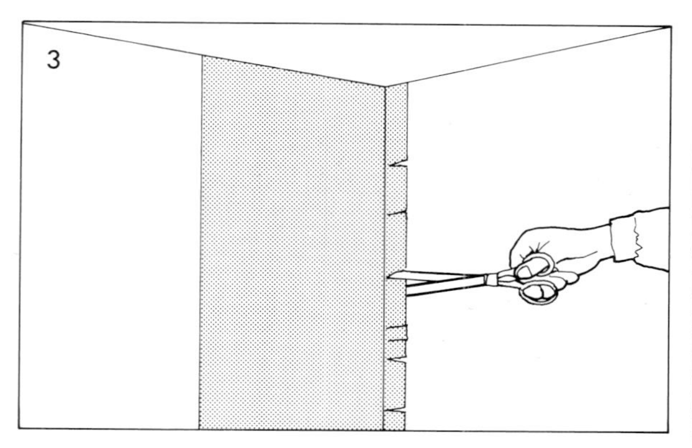

The overlap of paper will crease on a very uneven wall, so snip into it at each crease so that you can make it lie as flat as possible.

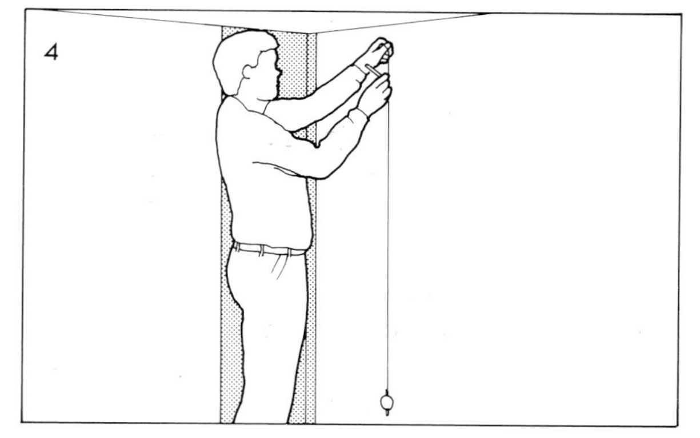

Measure out from the corner the width of the offcut from the previous roll plus 6 mm ($\frac{1}{4}$ in) and drop a plumbline at this point.

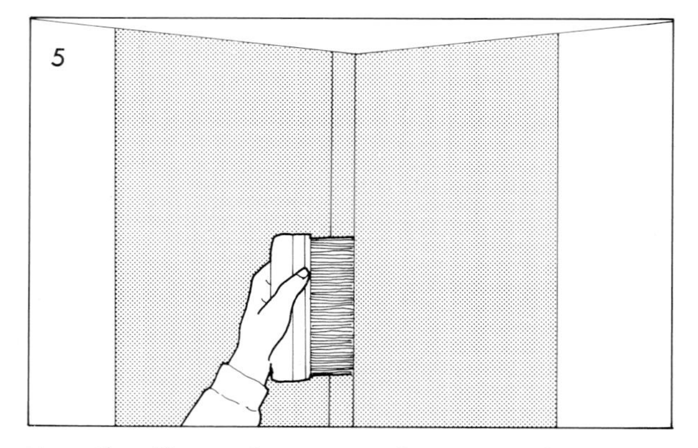

Hang the offcut on the return wall, its outer edge aligned with the plumbed line and the inner edge covering the overlap of the previous drop.

Papering External Corners

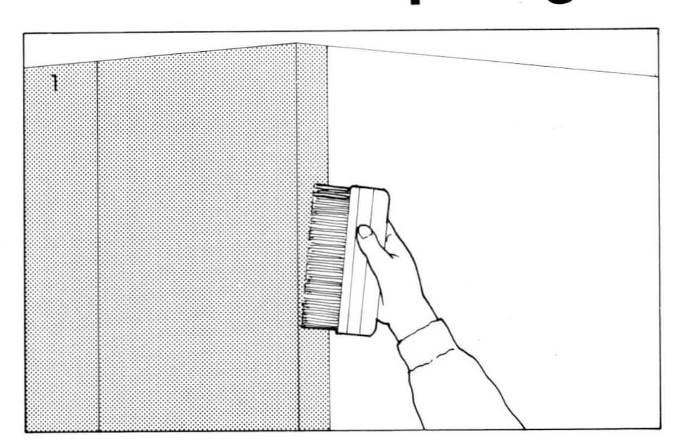

When papering around an external corner, turn no more than 25 mm (1 in) of paper onto the return wall and brush it as flat as possible.

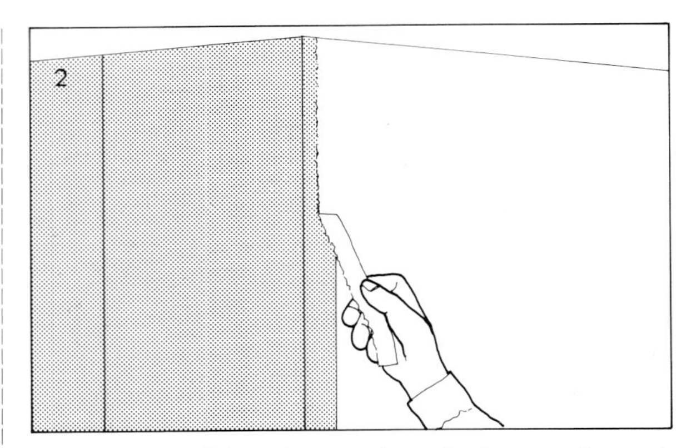

To avoid a harsh line showing through when overlapped by the subsequent drop, carefully tear down the overlap to create a soft, feathered edge.

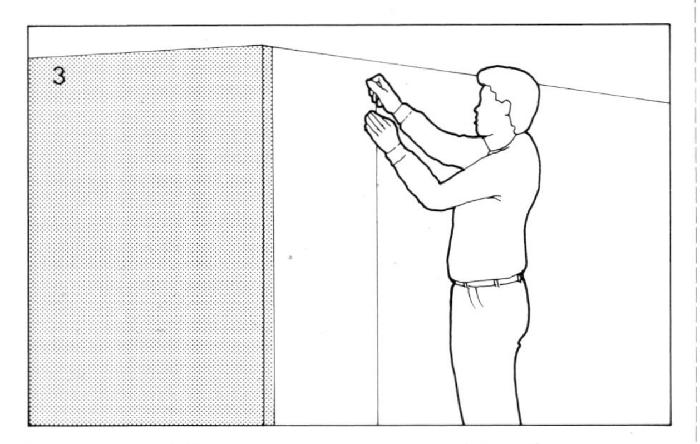

Drop a plumbline on the return wall a full roll width away from the corner, plus 6 mm ($\frac{1}{4}$ in), as a guide to hanging the next strip of wallpaper.

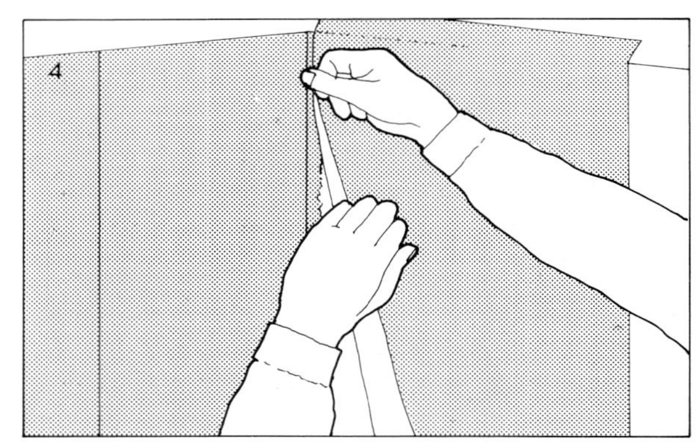

Hang the next full drop, aligning one edge with the plumbed line while the other edge overlaps the feathered edge of the previous overlap.

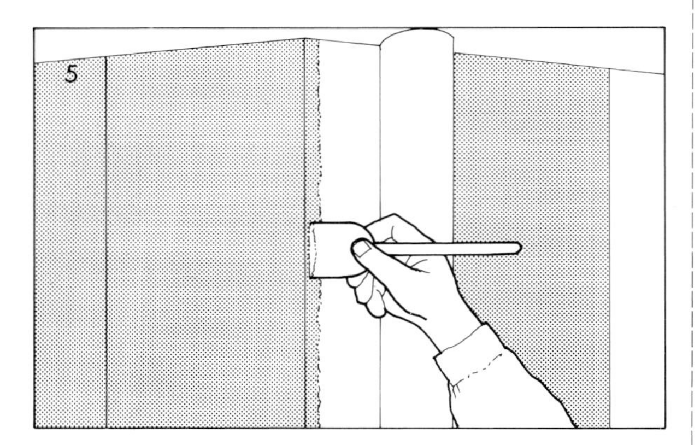

Vinyl wallcoverings will not adhere to themselves, so wherever you have to overlap edges you will have to use a latex adhesive.

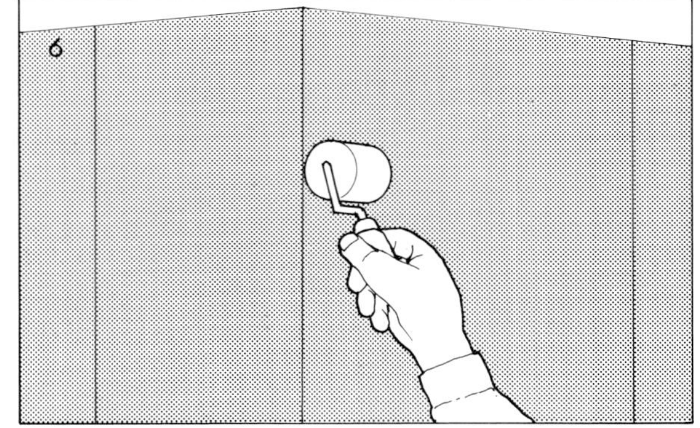

Run a seam roller along the external corner overlap to flatten down the double thickness of wallpaper and ensure the edges are stuck.

Papering Around Openings

All rooms will have at least one doorway and window to deal with when wallpapering. The precise hanging details depend on how close the door or window is to a corner, but the principles are the same. Take care during your initial setting out to plot the positions of the widths of wallpaper accurately.

It is usual to commence hanging wallpaper from the edge of a doorway. Hang the drop immediately before the doorway as normal, then hang the next full drop over the opening. Trim off the waste within the doorway, leaving about 25 mm (1 in) beyond the frame. Next, snip diagonally into the top corner about 6 mm ($\frac{1}{4}$ in) beyond the frame edge and use a paper-hanger's brush to tap the paper into the angle between the wall and the door frame. Score the overlap with the blade of your scissors, peel away the paper and cut off the waste neatly. Brush the paper back in place.

Complete widths of wallpaper are unlikely to fit exactly around the room, and there will be a slight mismatch of pattern where the last drop meets the edge of the first drop. Being a short drop above the door, and behind you as you enter the room, the break in pattern continuity will not be so noticeable. Allow the last short drop to overlap the first drop fractionally then carefully tear the flap to create a feather-edged join.

Papering around a flush window frame is tackled similarly to a doorway, although the small drops above and below the window must match the complete drops at each side. This means that you must cut them from a single long strip and waste the central section. Hang a complete drop over the window, score against the frame and trim to fit.

On a recessed window, pattern-matching is most important, because the window might be a focal point of the room. Hang a full-width drop over the opening so that it can be turned onto the reveal: cut across the paper at the soffit edge (underside of top of frame) and fold the paper onto the side reveal. Continue hanging short lengths above the window, turning them under the soffit: ensure that the short lengths below the window match the previously hung drop. Cut a small piece of wallpaper to fit at the end of the soffit, overlapping the reveal and face wall, and covered by the edge of the full drop.

Papering Archways

Archways are not difficult to paper around so long as you follow a basic procedure. Paper the walls on both sides of the archway first, allowing a 2.5 cm (1 in) overlap at the perimeter of the arch. Make a series of cuts in from the edge of the overlap every 2.5 cm (1 in), then fold the flaps over onto the soffit (underside of the arch).

Cut a strip of paper to fit the width of the arch, less a few centimetres at each side. Paste and soak the paper, then brush onto the soffit from the bottom up, then down around the other side.

Where the pattern of the paper would look wrong if it was upside down, paper the soffit with two strips joined at the top, overlapping the join and cutting through both with a sharp knife:

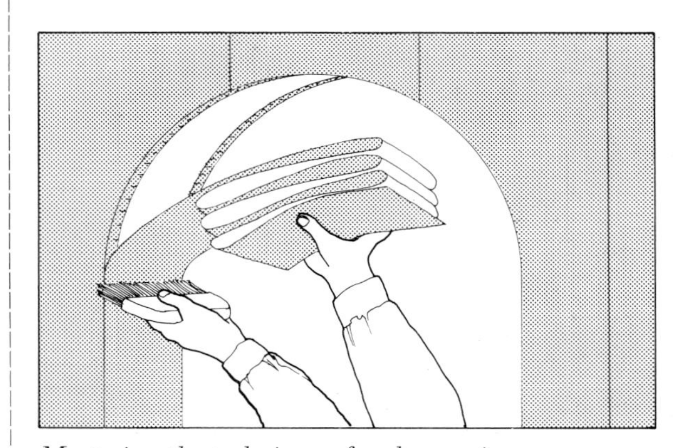

Mastering the technique of arch papering.

Papering Around Doors

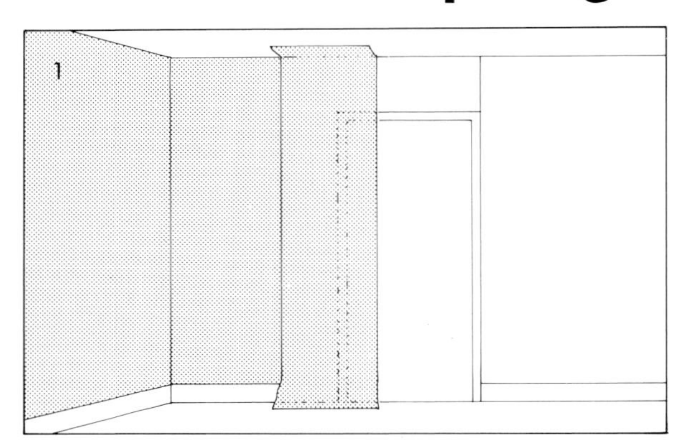

After hanging the last drop immediately before the doorway, hang the next one over the opening without brushing into the frame.

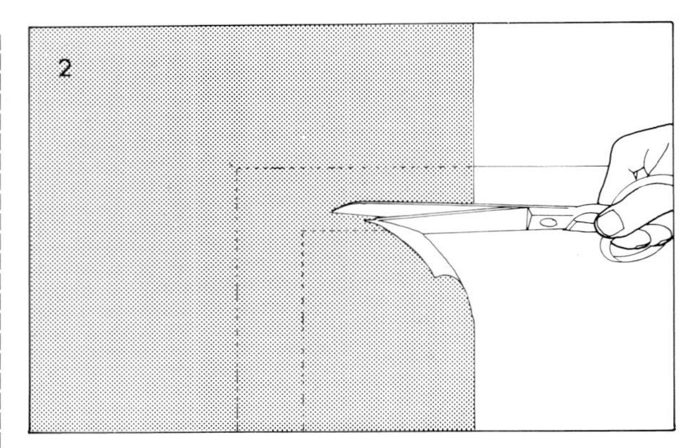

Using long-bladed scissors, trim back the waste paper in the door opening to within about 25 mm (1 in) of the outer edge of the architrave.

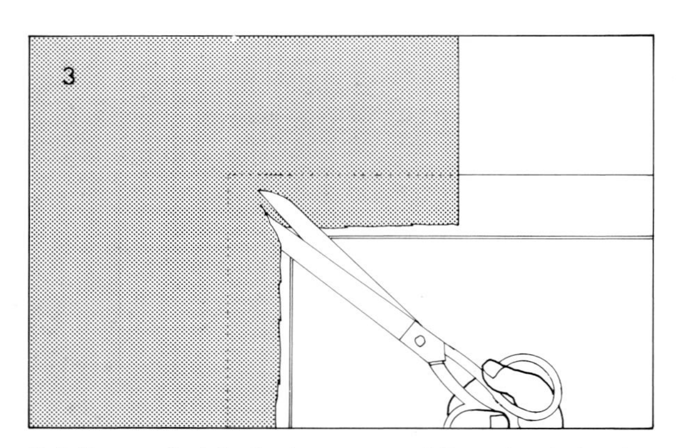

Cut diagonally into the top corner of the cut-out about 6 mm ($\frac{1}{4}$ in) beyond the edge of the frame so that the paper can be made to lie against the wall.

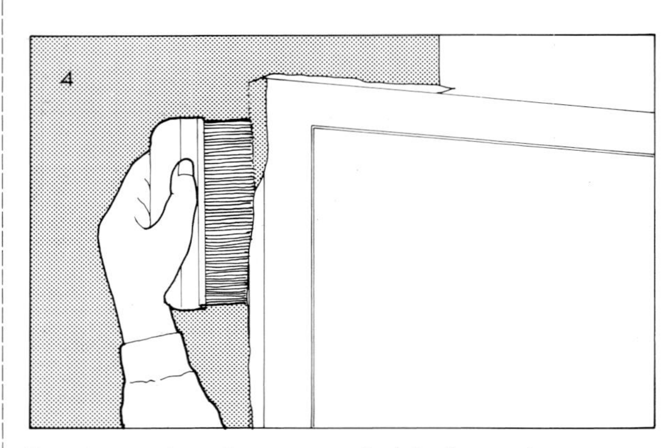

Tap the overlap of paper gently into the angle between the wall and the architrave using the bristles of the paperhanger's brush.

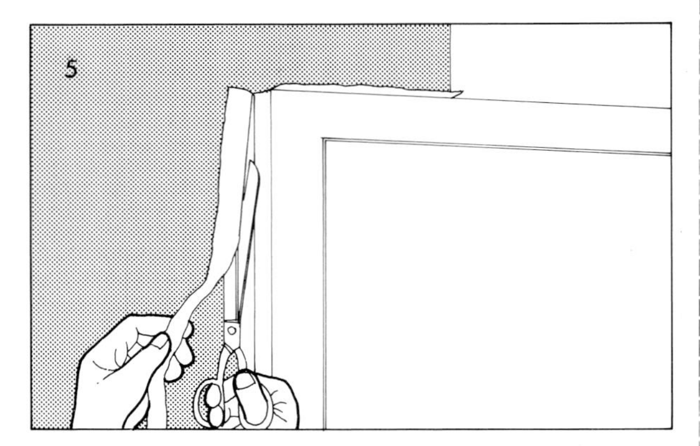

Score along the overlap in the architrave angle using the blade of your scissors, then peel away the paper and cut off the excess.

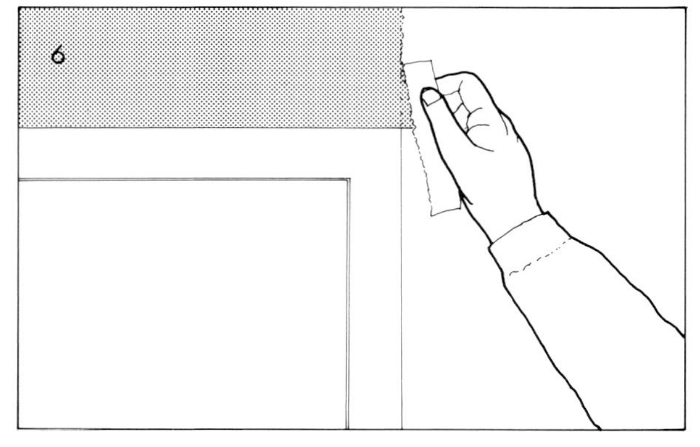

Where the last short drop over the doorway meets the edge of the first full drop, allow a slight overlap, then tear the edge to feather the join.

Papering Around Windows

On a flush window, hang a drop over the opening, cut out the waste then score and trim the edge around the architrave or frame edge.

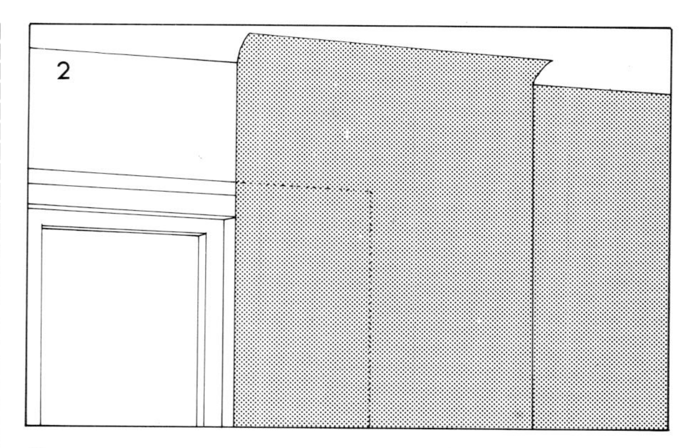

On a recessed window, hang a drop with its waste overlapping the soffit (underside) and reveal (side) of the window opening.

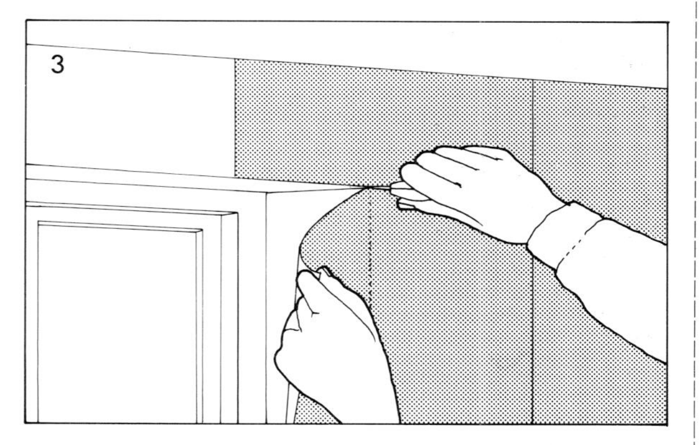

Using a sharp knife, cut along the soffit edge and turn the paper around onto the side reveal. Trim it into the edge of the window frame.

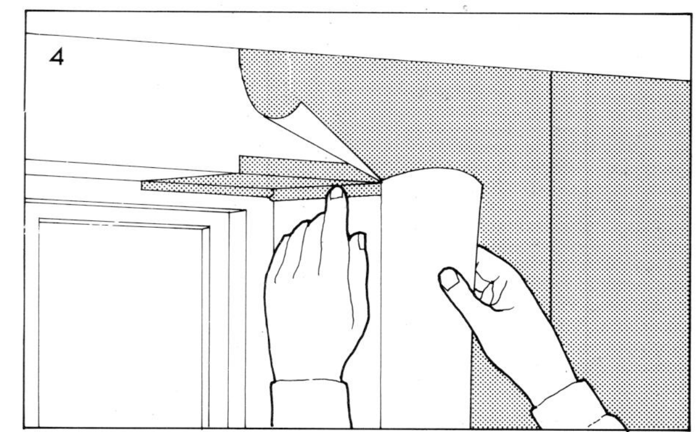

Hang short drops above and below the opening, matching the sides. Cut offcuts to fit the soffit ends, overlapping the wall face and reveal.

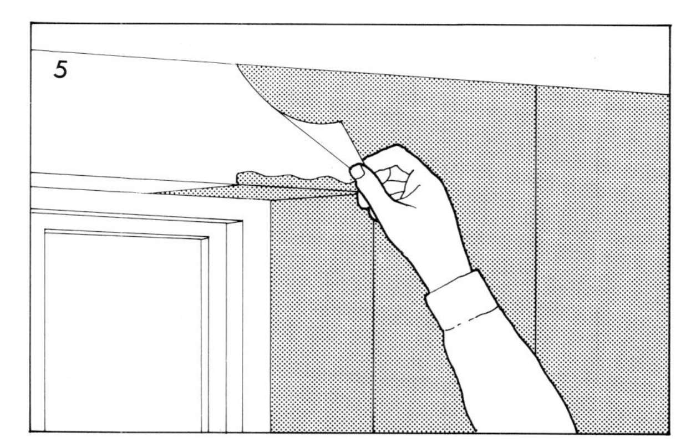

Cover the offcut's overlaps at reveal and soffit. Cut a wavy line through the face overlap, remove the offcut and brush back for a neat butt join.

Papering Ceilings and Stairwells

A ceiling is often wallpapered to conceal a bumpy, cracked or stained surface, although you can readily hang a patterned or embossed paper for decorative effect. Although more awkward to paper than walls, ceilings usually contain fewer obstructions – say a ceiling rose or a chimney breast to paper around. Safe access should be your priority when planning to decorate a ceiling: although you can manage with scaffold boards between pairs of stepladders you would be wiser to hire decorators' trestles, which are especially designed to suit this purpose and a far safer option.

Prepare the ceiling as for walls, then plot and mark out the runs of paper using stringlines stretched across the surface: chalk rubbed along the strings will transfer a guideline to the ceiling when the string is twanged against the surface.

Cut the paper and paste as normal, then fold concertina-fashion, leaving a broad fold at one end, and leave to soak. Supporting the paper on a spare roll in one hand, unfold the end and brush onto the ceiling with the other. Walk forwards across your platform, unfolding the paper and brushing it smoothly into place. Allow the paper to overlap the walls: crease into the corner, peel away and cut diagonally so that you can brush it back flat. If the walls are not going to be papered you can trim the overlaps later; otherwise the wallpaper can cover the overlaps.

When you come to a ceiling pendant light, first turn off the power at the mains, remove the shade and bulb and loosen the rose cover. Pierce the paper with scissors and feed the lampholder and flex through. Cut triangular flaps from the hole so the paper will lie flat against the ceiling, then trim around the rose.

At an alcove, hang the paper up to the obstruction and cut diagonally up to the corner, crease and trim each edge separately. Your last length is unlikely to be a full width: cut the paper roughly to size prior to pasting.

Stairwells present different problems when wallpapering; difficulty of access and the extremely long drops necessary – often twice as high as a room wall. Special stair ladders and scaffolding can be hired, which straddle the stairs but give you a flat working platform. It will probably be necessary, however, to erect a makeshift platform for the higher, more inaccessible parts. Use an arrangement of ladders, stepladders, scaffold boards – all securely lashed together – according to the layout of your stairwell.

To hang the paper, you will need assistance: while you position and brush on the paper from the top, your helper must support the heavy, concertina-folded drop below to prevent the paper from tearing. Hang the longest drop first, then work around the stairwell, finishing with the head wall of the stairwell. You will be forced to measure, cut and paste each drop one at a time, because each is shorter than the subsequent one: remember to measure the long edge at the angled stair skirting.

Papering a Ceiling

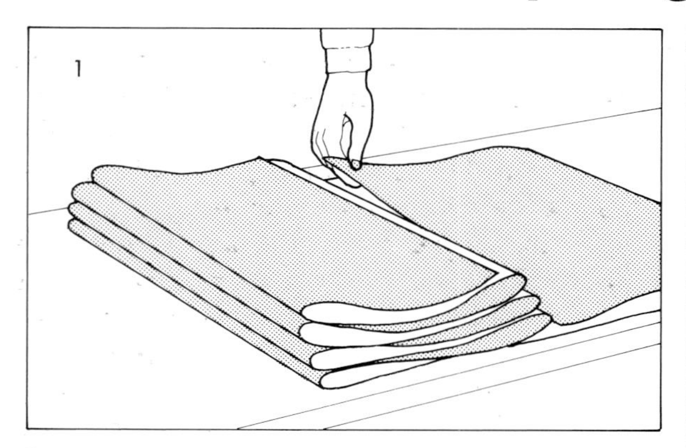

Paste the long length of paper and fold concertina-fashion to make it easier to carry; a 300 mm (12 in)-fold at one end is the section to hang first.

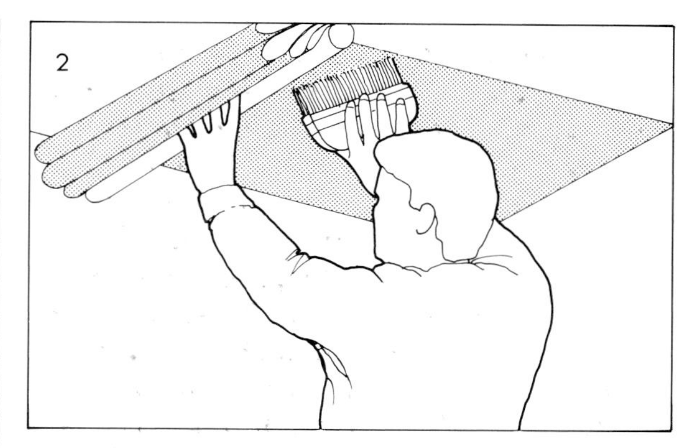

Face the wall, paper supported on a spare roll; unpeel the folded end and brush onto the ceiling, allowing overlaps onto the walls.

Brush the paper onto the ceiling, working across the room. At a ceiling pendant, pierce the paper and feed the lampholder and flex through.

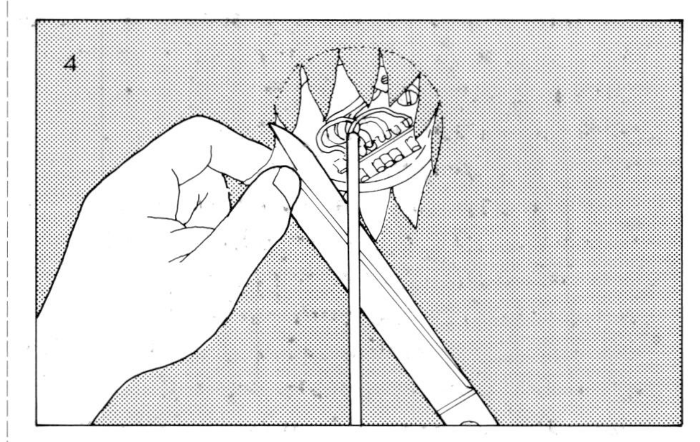

Cut triangular flaps around the pierced hole so that you can brush the paper flat onto the ceiling around the pendant rose; trim off the flaps.

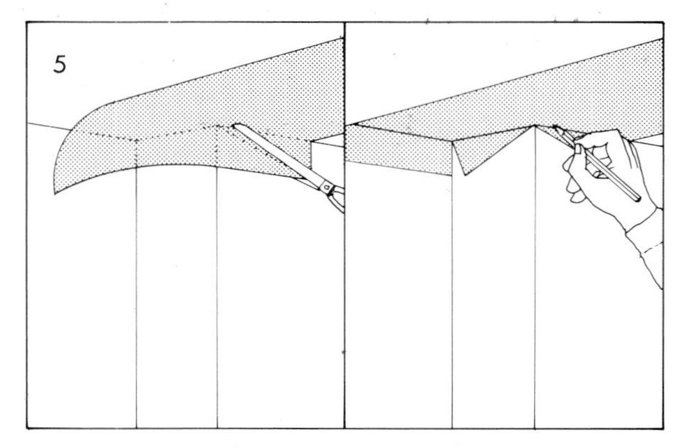

Where the length falls at the corner of an alcove, hang the paper up to the obstruction, cut diagonally to the corner, crease and trim each edge.

Papering a Stairwell

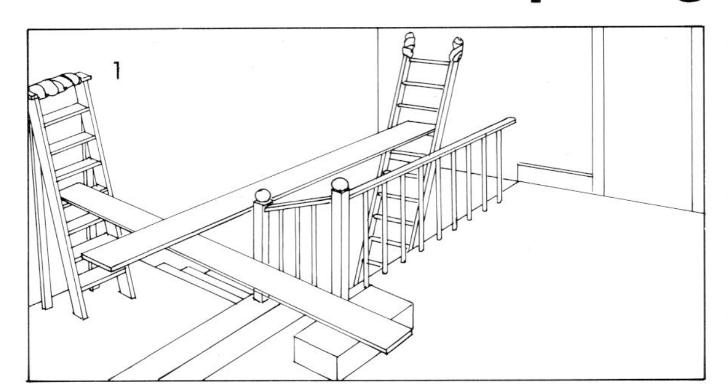

For access, set up ladders, steps, scaffold boards and a hop-up or stout box; lash together and pad the ladder ends to protect the walls.

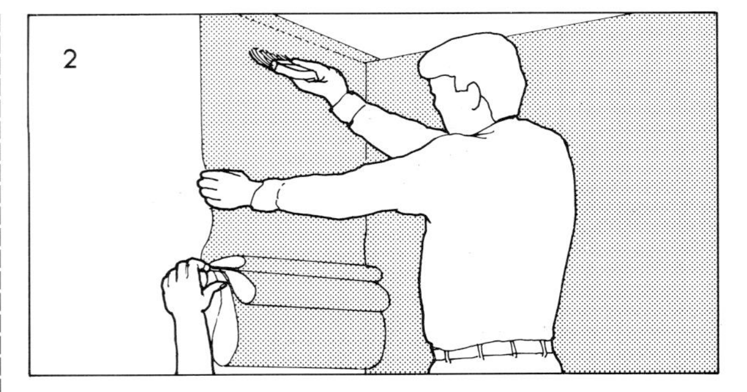

Start by hanging the longest drop, using a helper to support the folded paper below you to prevent it from tearing; treat as for walls.

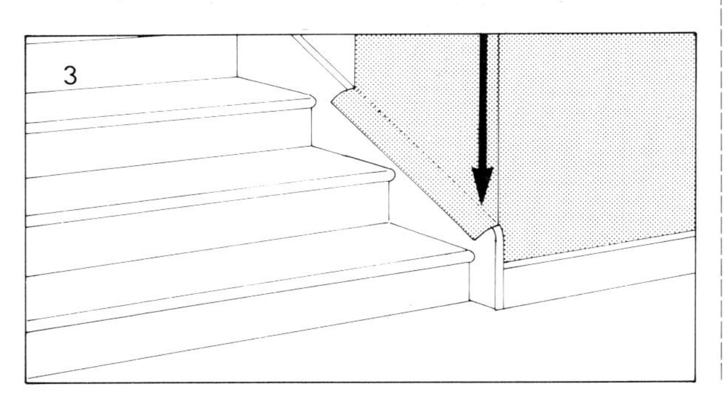

When measuring each drop, measure the long edge at the bottom of angled skirting. Allow overlaps at top and bottom and trim accordingly.

Hanging Relief Wallcoverings

Heavyweight relief wallcoverings such as woodchip and Anaglypta require different considerations when hanging. Although they will conceal minor imperfections, the surface must be clean, smooth and sound. It is best, therefore, to cross-line the walls with thick lining paper first (see page 100). The hanging procedure for straight drops is identical to that for ordinary papers, although you must be careful not to flatten the embossed pattern. Butt-join the edges of the drops, but do not worry unduly if there is a slight gap: because most coverings are intended to be painted, the gap will not be noticeable. Tap the butt join gently with the bristles of the paperhanger's brush but do not use a seam roller, which will flatten the emboss. Crease and trim the paper as normal.

Due to the thickness of embossed wallcoverings it is not advisable to overlap lengths at internal corners. Instead, turn a wide margin around the corner, crease and cut the paper to the wall profile, using a scalpel knife. Use the offcut, squared up to a new plumbline, to start the return wall, with the cut edges abutting. Dip a finger in some ready-mixed filler and run this down the corner to conceal the raw edge.

When using woodchip paper on external corners, overlap the drops then cut through the overlap, remove the offcut and press back the flaps to give a true butt-join.

Hanging Relief Papers

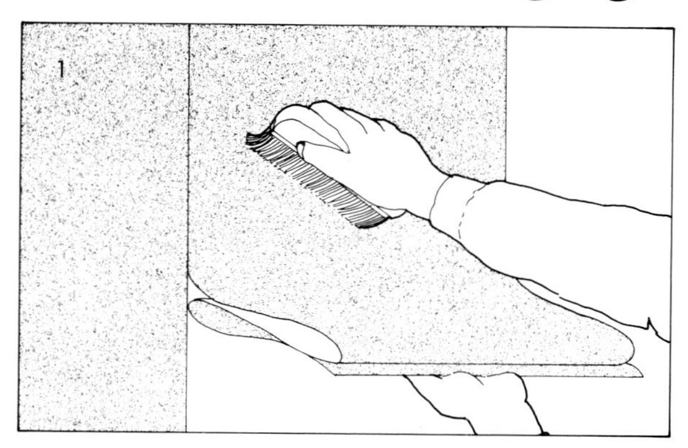

Relief coverings can be cut, pasted and left to soak as for ordinary papers. Hang straight drops in the same way, taking care not to flatten the emboss.

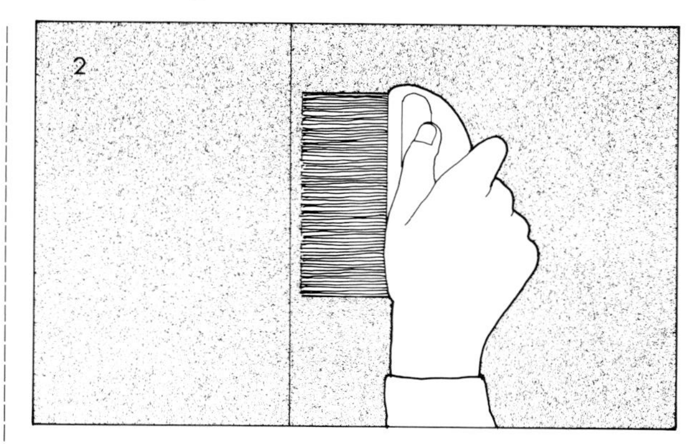

Butt-join straight drops of relief wallcovering and tap the edges gently with the paperhanger's brush to make sure they are properly stuck.

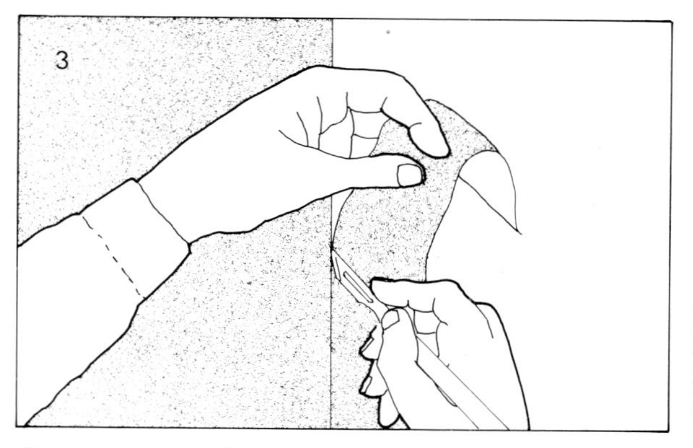

Turn a wide margin around a corner, crease and cut it to the wall profile, then align the offcut with a plumbline to start the return wall.

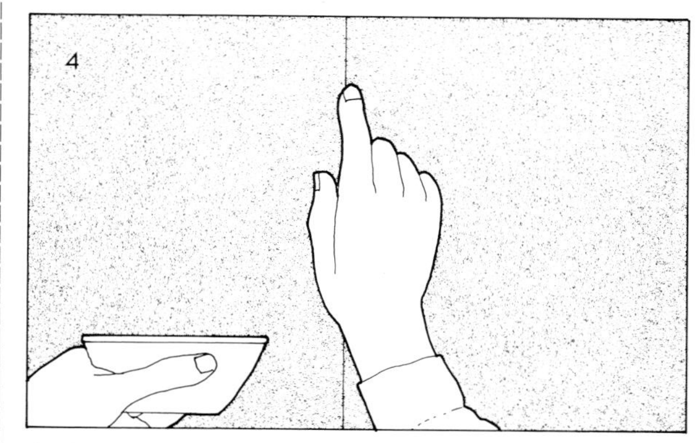

As the wallcovering will be painted, you can conceal the raw edge of the meeting drops with filler applied on a fingertip.

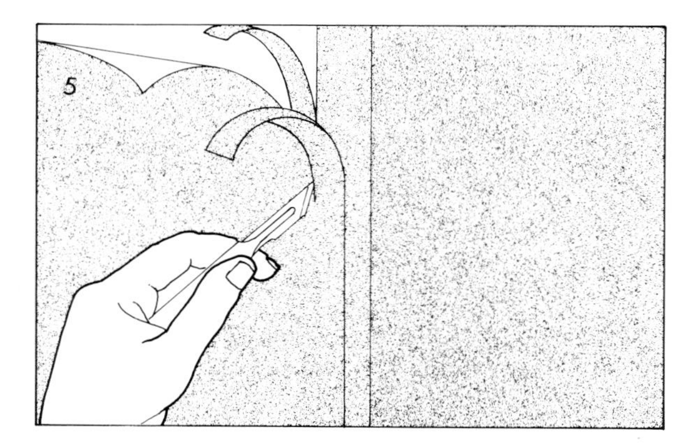

When using woodchip paper at an external corner, overlap the drops then cut through both and peel off the waste, then brush back the flaps.

Hanging Lincrusta

The method of hanging this heavy-weight wallcovering is basically straightforward, but its sheer weight and inflexibility make it unwieldy. Rolls and dados are hung in basically the same way – by applying a thick glue to the backing paper – although the ready-trimmed panels are marginally easier to work with. The instructions here apply specifically to hanging dado panels, but virtually the same sequence applies to hanging floor-to-ceiling drops. However, whereas panels are ready-trimmed, rolls have a selvedge which must be trimmed off prior to hanging. Additionally, rolls must be pattern-matched on each length and the individual lengths cut with a few extra inches for trimming at top and bottom.

Lincrusta tends to highlight even minor imperfections in a wall surface, which would also give a poor bond, so always double cross-line the walls with lining paper. First hang the vertical lengths, then hang horizontal strips over the top. This provides a thick, flat layer and an excellent base for the Lincrusta.

Measure the height of a dado panel – 914 mm (36 in) – and mark a pencil line on the wall this distance up from the skirting board. Mark the dado height on the wall at the other end of the run then draw a horizontal line linking the marks, using a long spirit level as a rule. Set up your pasting table, then carry three or four panels to the table ready for glueing. Grip near the corners of one end in both hands and lift smoothly without bending the panel or the surface may craze. Carry vertically, lay down the bottom edge carefully then lower to the surface, face-down. Before gluing, make sure the panels are the same length – some panels from different batches might be slightly longer than others.

Sponge the back of the panels generously with clean, warm water and leave to soak for about 20 to 30 minutes. Soaking fully expands the Lincrusta and helps to prevent bubbles forming during hanging. After soaking, wipe the back of each panel with a dry cloth to remove surplus water then apply the Lincrusta glue. The glue is supplied with a thick consistency like wax polish. Stir thoroughly until it reaches a stiff but workable consistency like honey. Apply the glue to the panels with an old 70 or 100 mm (3 or 4 in)-wide paintbrush. Make sure you coat the back of the panel fully, swirling the glue onto the surface quite liberally. Pay attention to the edges, which are fairly stiff and tend to curl back unless well-glued. You can apply the glue with a paint roller, by pouring it into a roller tray.

Carry the first panel to the wall and press against the surface, aligning the top edge with the pencilled guidelines. The lower edge of the panel should run along the top of the skirting board. However, if the skirting is not level you can trim the panel later with a sharp knife: for perfect symmetry it's best to align the dado with the horizontal guideline. Smooth the panel onto the wall with a cloth pad or use a 100 mm (4 in)-wide rubber roller. Ensure that all parts of the panel are firmly struck.

Apply glue to the second panel and position on the wall, butting its edge tight against the previously hung panel. Remove any surplus using a damp sponge.

Carry on hanging panels until you reach the end of the wall, or a doorway. Measure the gap between the last-hung panel and the corner, or architrave, at top, middle and bottom then transfer these dimensions to the face of another panel. Draw a pencil line down the panel, linking the marks, and trim off the waste with a sharp trimming knife held against a metal straightedge. Ensure that you keep the knife blade pressed against the straightedge as you cut: the blade may tend to wander at the thicker parts of the emboss and it's essential that the cut is clean to ensure a neat edge. Glue the trimmed panel and stick on the wall.

Packs of dado panels come with a roll of moulded border, about 25 mm (1 in) wide, which fits along the top edge of the dado. Measure the length of the run and cut the border to match. Apply glue to the back and press the border in place.

The dado panels can be continued from a hallway up a stairway, although some pattern mismatch is inevitable. The rigid Art Nouveau and Edwardian designs appear quite drastically offset until you see the run in its entirety. Mark a vertical plumbline at the base of the stairs and repeat at the top of the stairs. Mark the height of a panel on the plumblines up from the string (skirting), and at intervals. Draw a diagonal line linking the marks, which runs parallel with the string.

To give you a template for cutting the dado panels to the correct rake, start by cutting a panel lengthways in half with a sharp knife. Then cut a piece of cardboard – use a packing box – to match one half. Place a long edge of the card against the plumbed line at the base of the stairway and align the top corner with the height indication. Mark on the card the point on the opposite side at the edge of the skirting. Join the corner up to this mark and cut across the line. You now have your template.

Place the template on the lower edge of the half-panel and cut across the hypotenuse. Set aside the triangular offcut: do not dispose of it. Apply glue to the half-panel then hang it on the stairway, aligning the angled lower edge with the staircase string. Glue the triangular piece cut from the base of the panel on the top of the panel, aligning it with the sloping guideline. Cut, glue and hang the other half of the panel. Continue hanging half-panels up the stairway, then proceed along the landing with full panels. Cut, glue and fit border strips as before to finish the stairway dado.

Never attempt to turn panels – or rolls – of Lincrusta around external or internal corners, unless these are rounded, as the emboss would crack unevenly. Measure and cut the wall-covering to finish at the angle and butt up lengths. When cutting, hold the knife blade at an angle so that a mitre is cut: at an external corner undercut the edges so they will meet neatly; at an internal corner, slope the blade the other way.

Hanging Lincrusta Panels

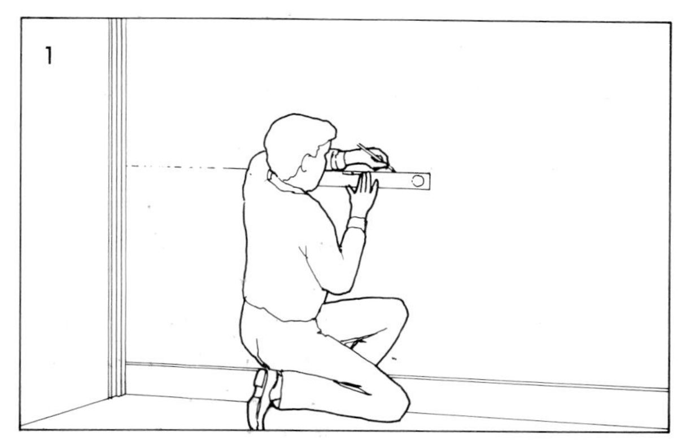

Having prepared and cross-lined the walls, the dado height is marked up. The back of the panel must be soaked first, before the special Lincrusta glue is applied.

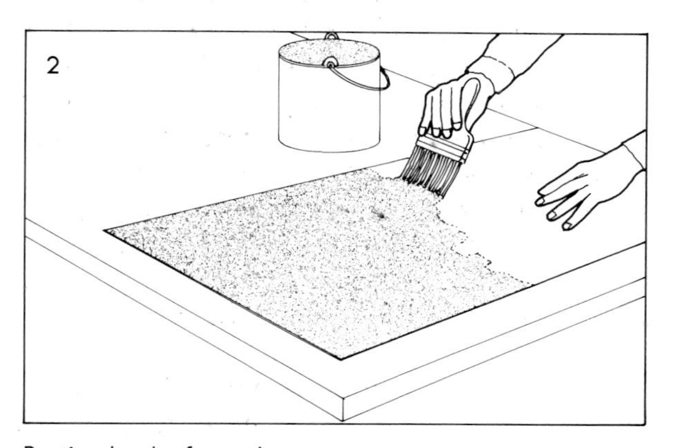

Pasting back of panel

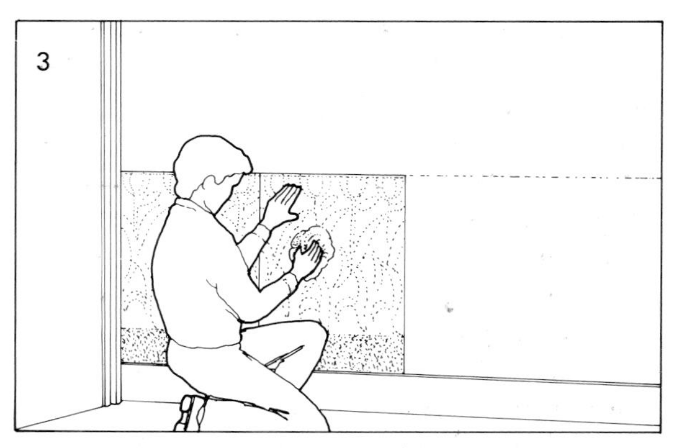

Smoothing on panel with rag.

(Continued on page 116)

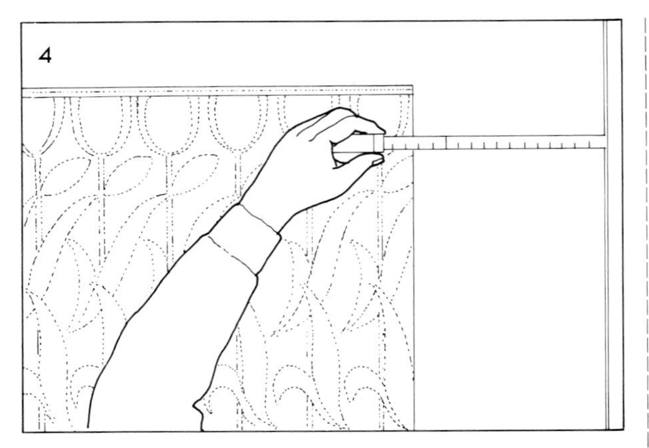

Measuring the width of the last panel.

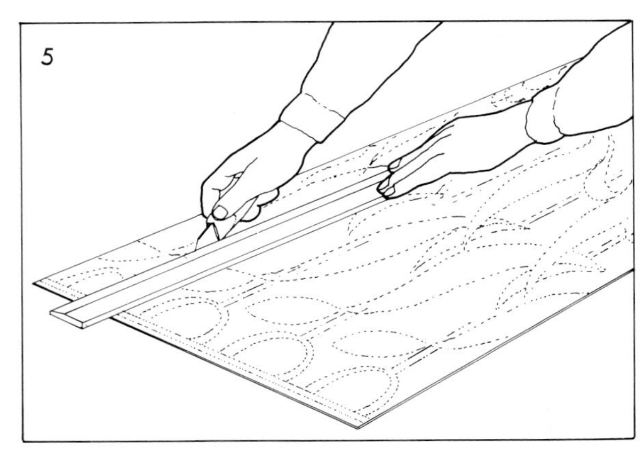

Trimming with a sharp knife.

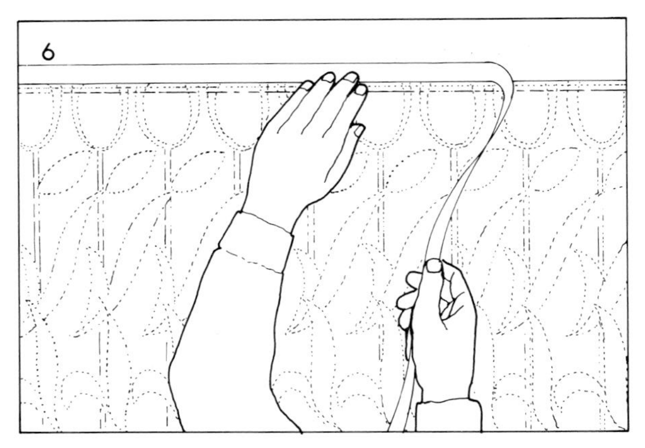

Cut and fit the pre-formed top trim.

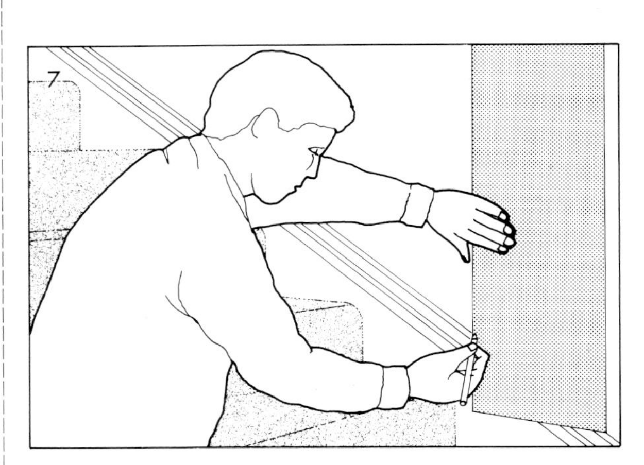

Marking the angle of the staircase using a cardboard template.

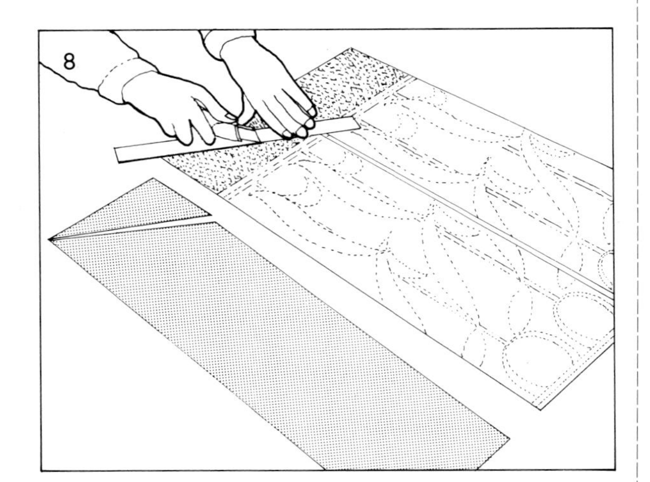

Trimming panel cut in two pieces for stairwell fitting.

Glue the triangular piece from the base of the stairway panel to the top, aligning it with the sloping guideline.

Hanging Fabric Wallcoverings

For all the numerous types of wall fabrics available – hessian, felt, grasscloth, suede, silkcloth, cork, wool, linen – the method for hanging is similar. Many fabrics are paper-backed and these are the easiest to work with as the unbacked types tend to distort. Whichever you choose, opt for the widest fabric you can find because it is preferable to have as few joins as possible. Prepare the walls as for ordinary wallcoverings (see page 94) and, especially if you are using unbacked fabrics, cross-line the surface (see page 100).

With unbacked fabrics, cut the lengths required, allowing for overlaps at the top and bottom of the wall, then roll it, face-in, onto a broom handle: without this support the fabric would be floppy and awkward to handle. Using the paste recommended by the supplier, brush onto the wall with light, feathered strokes for even coverage. While the paste is wet, unroll the fabric onto the wall, aligned with a plumbed line. Run a clean paint roller over the surface of the fabric to smooth it down evenly. Do not use a cloth pad as this distorts weaving.

Hang the second length of fabric so that it overlaps the first by about 25 mm (1 in), then cut vertically through the overlap with a sharp trimming knife held against a steel rule. Peel back the edges of the drops and pull out the offcuts of fabric, then smooth back the pieces and run a seam roller along the butt-join, taking care not to crush any pile.

Do not trim the overlaps at the top and bottom of the wall until the adhesive is dry and any shrinkage is complete. Trim off with a sharp knife.

If you have a particularly wide and heavy fabric, it's sensible to support it on a batten of wood spanning a pair of stepladders. Place the fabric on the wall from the bottom upwards.

With backed fabrics it's usual to paste the paper backing rather than the wall, as with ordinary wallcoverings. Use a soft paint roller to apply the adhesive rather than a brush.

Hanging Unbacked Fabrics

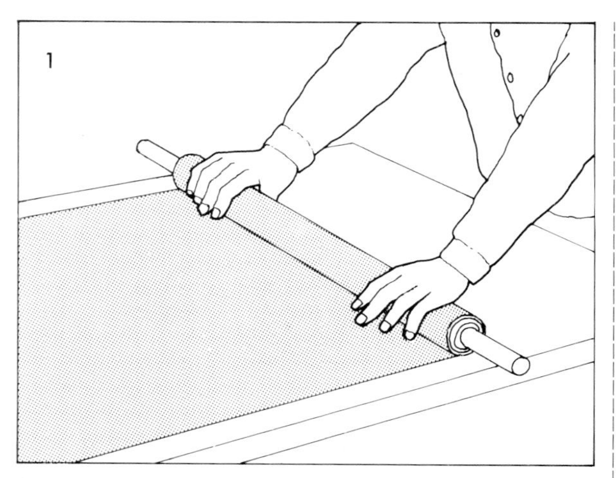

Cut the unbacked fabric to length plus 100 mm (4 in) each end for trimming, then roll, face-in, onto a broom handle for easier handling.

Apply the adhesive to the wall using a wide paintbrush. Apply enough to hang one drop and ensure that the entire surface is coated with adhesive.

(Continued on page 118)

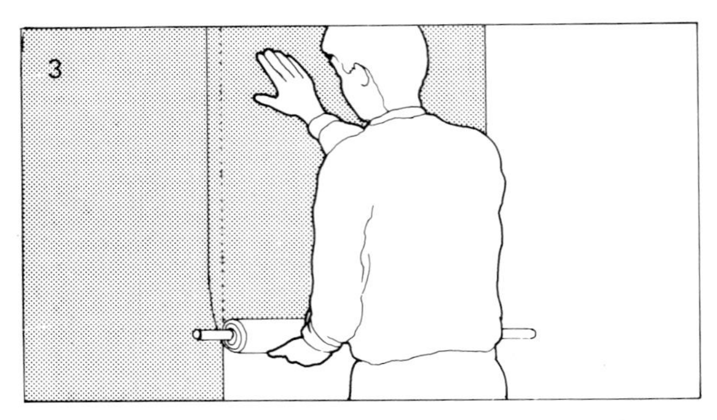

While the paste is still wet, unroll the fabric onto the wall, aligning it with a plumbed guideline, and smooth out with a clean, dry roller.

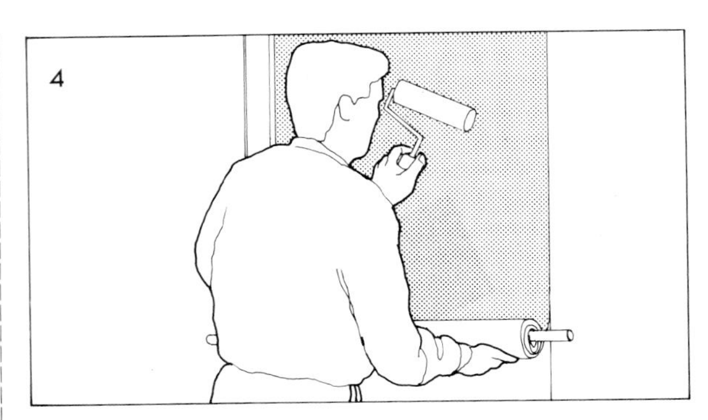

Cut, roll up and hang the second drop of fabric on the pasted wall, overlapping the edge of the first drop by about 25 mm (1 in).

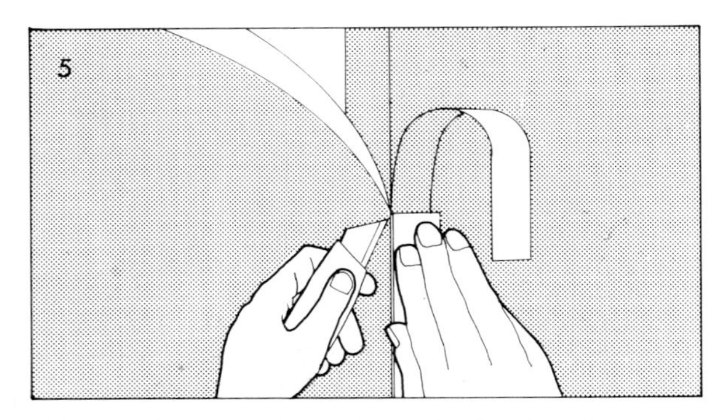

Cut through the overlap between the two lengths using a sharp knife held against a steel rule; remove the offcut and smooth back the edges.

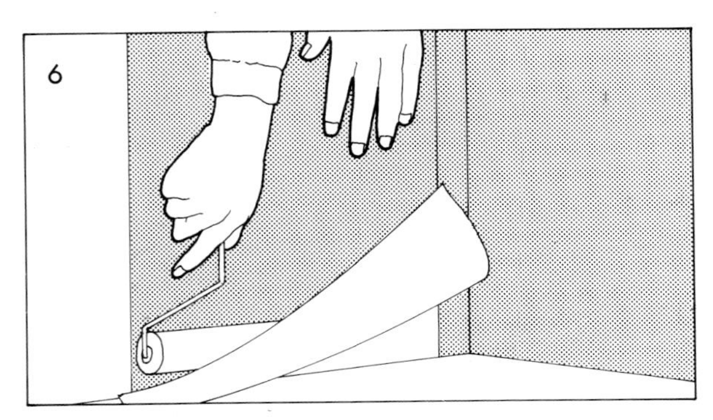

Turn around the corners by 50 mm (2 in); lap the next drop onto it by 25 mm (1 in). When the glue is dry, cut through both layers, peel off and restick.

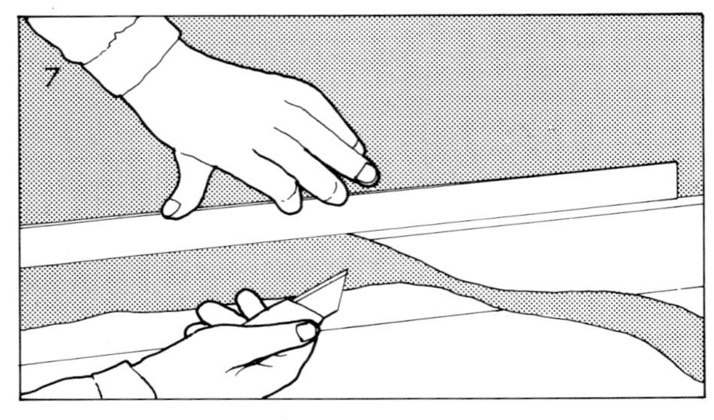

When the adhesive is dry and any shrinkage has ceased, trim the excess from the top and bottom of the wall using a sharp knife and straightedge.

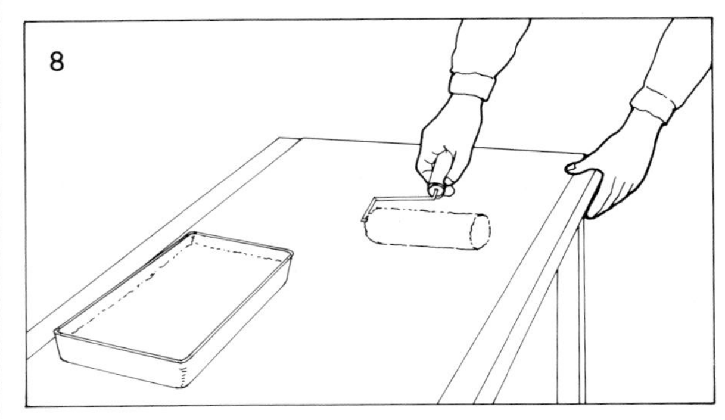

With backed fabrics you can apply the adhesive to the backing rather than the wall, using a soft paint roller to ensure complete coverage.

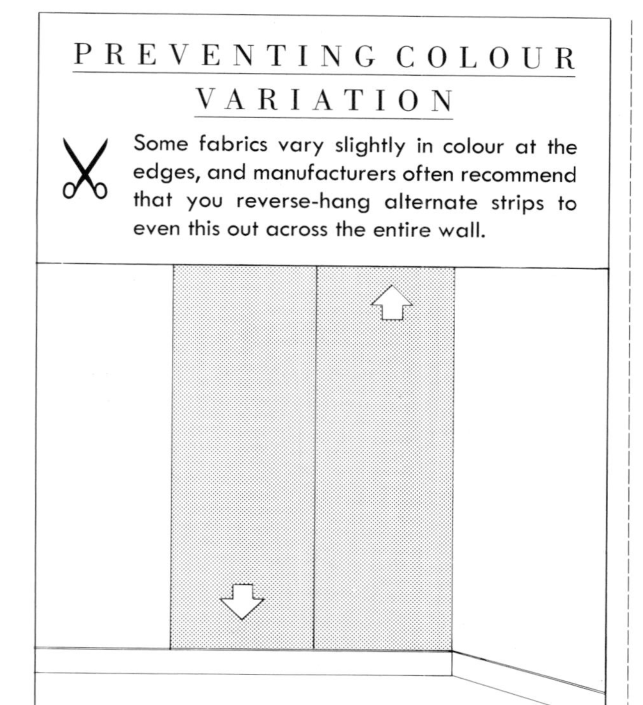

PREVENTING COLOUR VARIATION

Some fabrics vary slightly in colour at the edges, and manufacturers often recommend that you reverse-hang alternate strips to even this out across the entire wall.

SUPPORTING HEAVY FABRIC

Large, heavy rolls of fabric should be rolled onto a timber batten and supported between stepladders. Stick the fabric on the wall from the bottom up.

Making Fabric Wall Panels

Rigid fabric panels have the benefit of concealing poor walls, ugly pipes and electrical conduits. They can be used with delicate fabrics that cannot ideally be stuck to a wall – say dress fabrics, or those that would be likely to stretch, sag and be difficult to pattern-match. The best fabric to choose is medium-weight and tautly woven, with a glazed surface, or one that won't encourage dust. The fabric must be colourfast, shrink-resistant and, if it is a natural fibre, moth-proofed.

The rigid panels are made from 9 or 12 mm ($\frac{3}{8}$ or $\frac{1}{2}$ in)-thick, flame-retardant medium board (LM type, as used for pinboards), which comes in a 2.4 × 1.2 m (8 × 4 ft) standard size. Cut the panels to size with a panel saw and cut the fabric of your choice about 50 mm (2 in) larger all round than the panel. Spread the fabric face-down on the floor and lay a panel on top. Fold over the extra fabric and temporarily pin onto the back of the panel. Prepare several panels in this way, matching patterns. Pleat the fabric on the face of the panel (which will help disguise joins between panels) or stretch it taut.

Remove the pins from one long edge of the panel and apply latex adhesive to the fabric. Fold back the overlap and staple the fabric at regular intervals, stretching it evenly. Repeat for the other long edge, then the two narrow ends. Fold the corner flaps into mitres and staple.

Attach the panels to the wall using wallboard adhesive spread onto the surface, or secure with masonry nails or screws. You will have to conceal the heads of the fixings, perhaps with braid, which you can also stick along the joins between panels.

Making Fabric-covered Panels

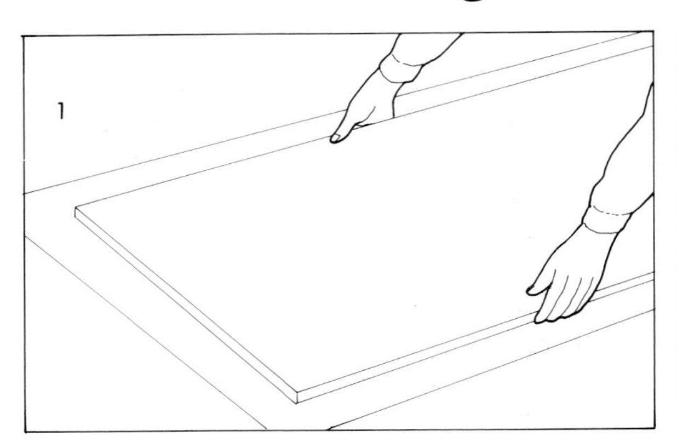

Cut the fabric and the board to size and lay the fabric face-down on the floor. Place the board squarely on top and secure the overlap with pins.

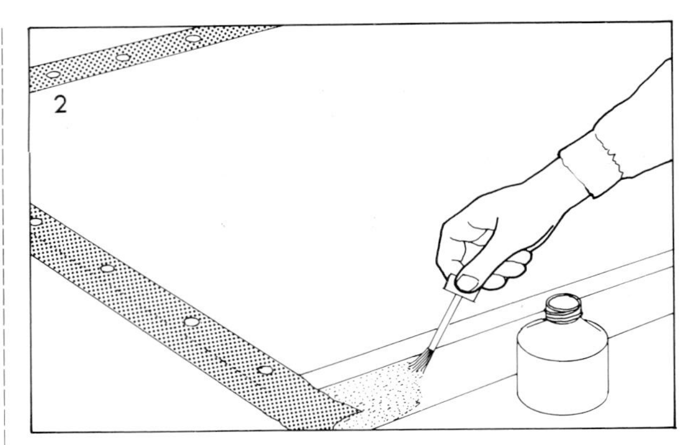

Make up several panels, pattern-matching as necessary. Remove the pins from a long edge and apply latex adhesive to the fabric overlap.

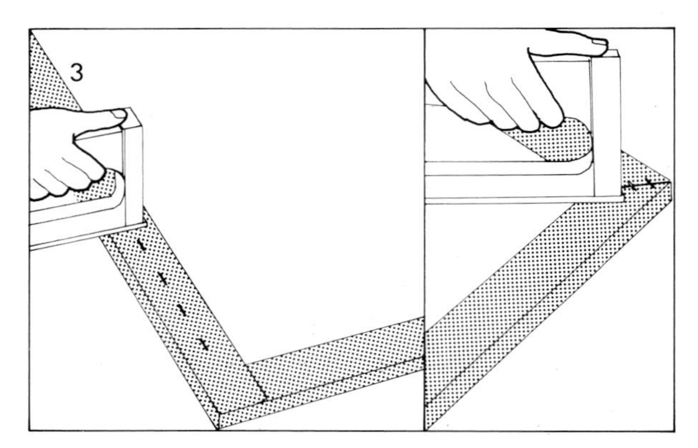

Stretch the fabric overlap evenly along the edge and secure at close, regular intervals with staples fired from a heavy-duty staple gun.

Attach the panels directly to the wall using a wallboard adhesive spread on in broad vertical bands. To secure, firmly press in place.

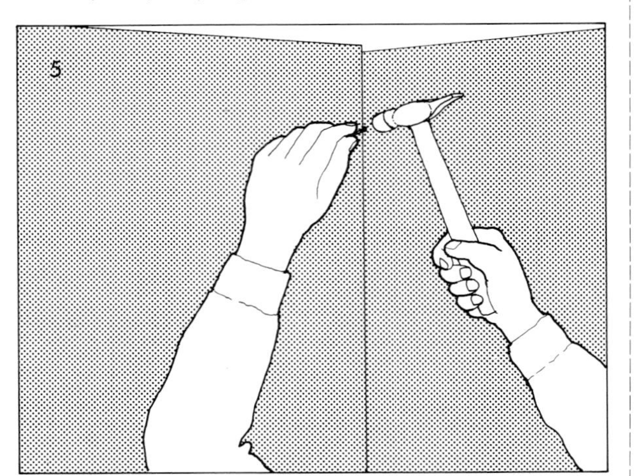

Alternatively, fix the rigid panels to the wall with non-rusting screws driven into wallplugs, or masonry nails hammered in.

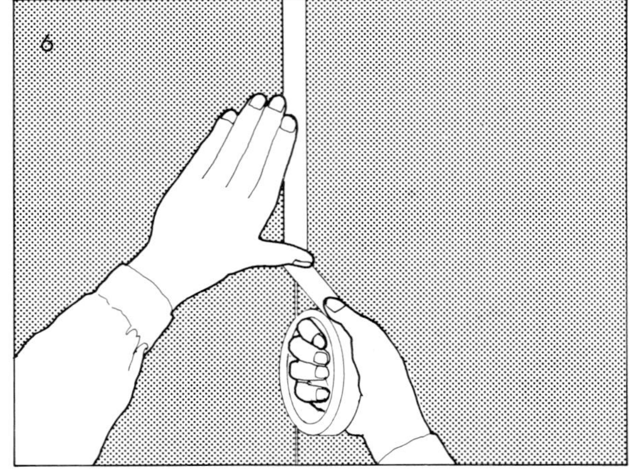

Braid can be stuck with latex adhesive along the vertical butt joins between wall panels, or used to disguise nails or screws.

Stick-on *Trompe L'Oeil*

Pre-cut *trompe l'oeil* wall decorations hand-printed on fine paper can, with imagination, be used to enhance a painted or papered surface. The designs typically offer fabric-like swags, tails and drops, with numerous rosettes, bows, cords, tassles, knots and cherub figures, to complete the effects. The pieces can be stuck to most wallpapers and painted surfaces using ordinary wallpaper paste or border adhesive, but will not readily adhere to textured surfaces.

Work out the positions of the pieces before pasting, perhaps by temporarily sticking them in place. If you are running a border of swags around a room, measure the walls to determine how many you will need and what spaces you will need to leave between them; if the gaps are too wide to be filled by rosettes or knots, overlap the swags and cover the overlap with the other features. Swags should always finish at the corners and the edges should be concealed with a rosette or other feature.

Paste the back of the pieces carefully, avoiding smearing the faces, then position on the wall. Wipe off any paste that squeezes from behind the piece with a damp rag. Run a seam roller gently over the surface to press the edges down.

Framing a Picture

Decide on the position of the picture then temporarily place the swags. Remove one by one, paste and stick on using a sponge to smooth down.

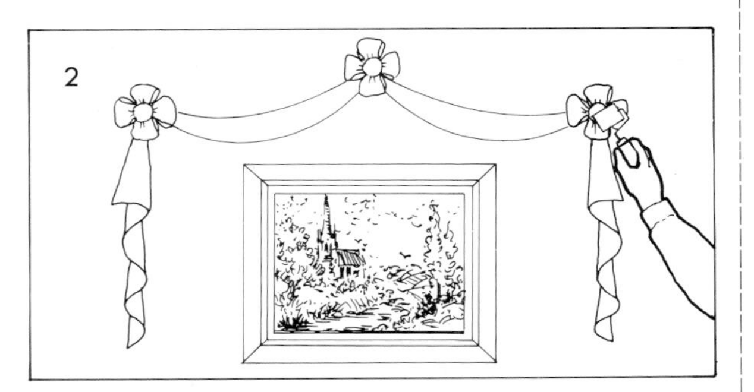

Stick on the rosettes so that they cover the gaps or overlaps between the swags, then press down firmly with a seam roller.

TREATING AN ENTIRE ROOM

For an overall effect, stick rope or swags around the ceiling/wall angle, as friezes, down corners and across the ceiling.

Hanging Friezes and Borders

Borders and friezes – narrow strips of patterned or embossed paper – are used to help improve the proportions of a room, to decoratively conceal the join at the top of a wall, or to emphasize a feature such as a dado rail, picture rail or staircase.

The most basic type of frieze is hung in the same way as ordinary wallpaper: the back is pasted and, after a soaking period, the paper is brushed onto the wall. Some types come ready-pasted and need only water to activate the adhesive, while others require you to paste the wall instead.

Mark the position of the frieze on the wall by marking where its bottom edge will be. Use a wooden batten and a spirit level as a guide to drawing a horizontal line around the room. Cut the frieze to length, apply paste to the back then fold concertina-fashion. If you are pasting the wall, the frieze can be applied direct from the roll.

Position the frieze and brush in place or (with pre-pasted types) smooth on with a damp, clean sponge. Trim the frieze squarely at a corner or other obstruction. Where you need to join two lengths of frieze midway along a wall, but the square-cut ends together, ensuring that the pattern matches.

To create a bordered panel-effect on a wall, stick on the strips as before, aligned with a pencil guideline, but mitre the corners neatly for continuity of pattern. At a right-angled corner, overlap the strips then slice diagonally through both layers and peel off the offcuts. Where the bordered panel follows the line of a stairway, the mitred cuts will not be right-angles, but follow the same cutting procedure for flow of pattern.

Hanging a Pasted Frieze

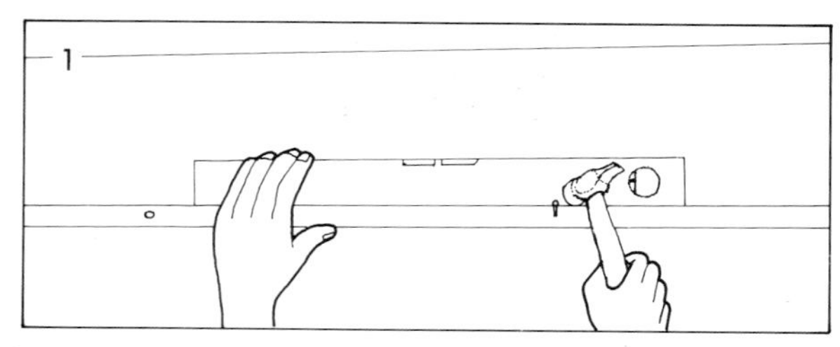

Measure down the wall and mark where the base of the frieze will be, then use a batten, spirit level and pencil to draw a line around the room.

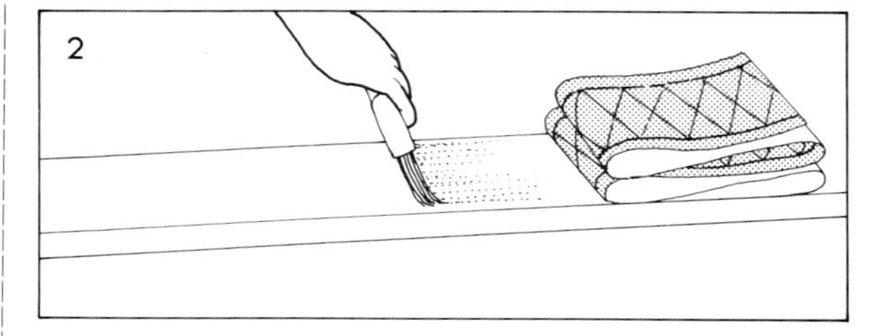

Cut the frieze to length, allowing extra for trimming at the corners, then paste the back and fold concertina-fashion and leave to soak.

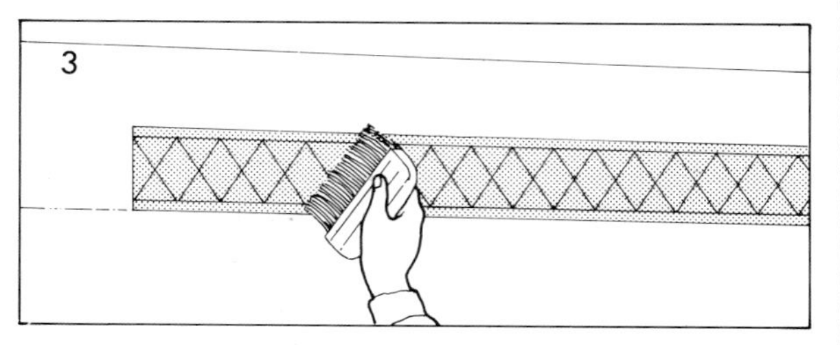

Position the frieze on the wall, aligned with the pencil guideline. Unfold it as you brush it into place, working across the wall.

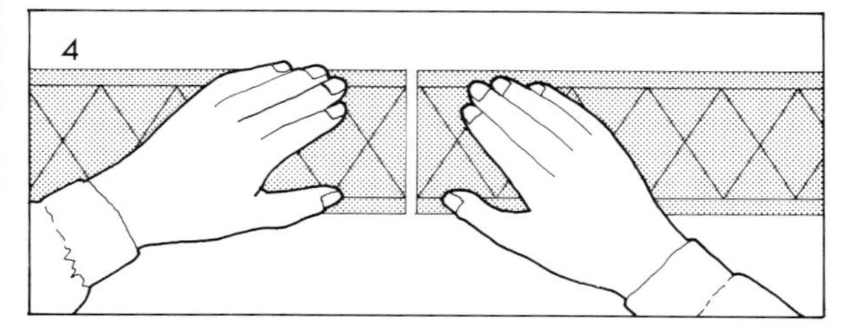

On long walls you might have to join straight lengths of freize. Cut the ends squarely and butt together, making sure that the pattern matches.

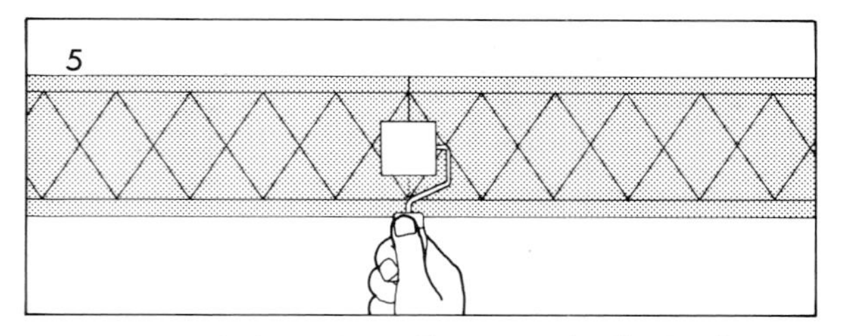

Use a damp cloth to wipe off smears of adhesive from the face and edges of the frieze, then use a wallpaper seam roller to flatten the joins.

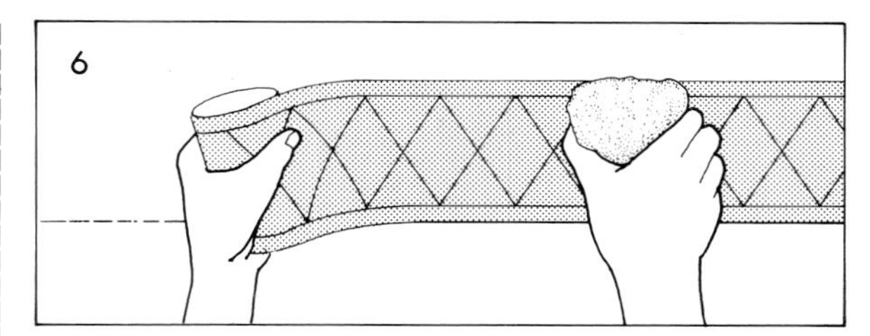

With paste-the-wall types mark twin horizontal lines the width of the frieze, apply paste then unroll the frieze on the wall and smooth with a damp sponge.

Making Bordered Panels

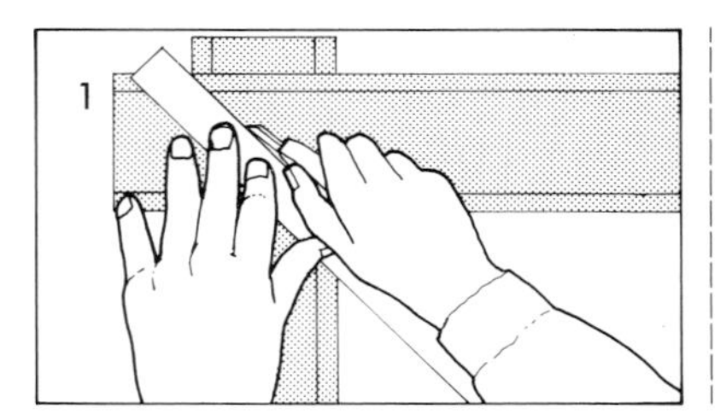

To form a bordered panel on a wall, overlap the frieze strips at the corners then slice diagonally through both layers with a scalpel and rule.

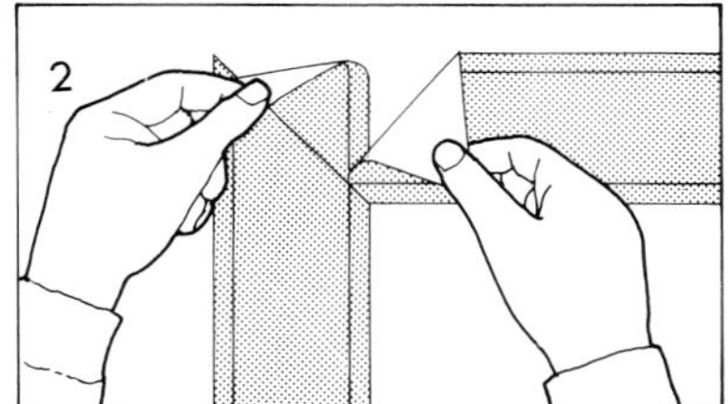

When corners are not right-angles – say where the frieze is taken up a stairway – use the same trimming technique for continuity of pattern.

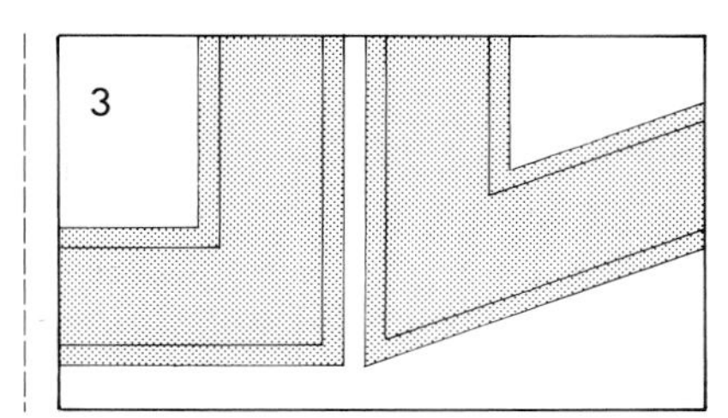

Peel back the overlapping strip of frieze and remove the offcut underneath. Smooth back the frieze to form a neat mitred join.

Decorating Relief Wallcoverings

Whites such as woodchip, and embossed coverings such as Anaglypta, used on walls and ceilings, are commonly decorated in a uniform colour using matt or silk emulsion. Once the covering has dried completely you can apply the paint using a roller. Before tackling the main area, however, use a 50 mm (2 in)-wide paintbrush to paint a margin around the ceiling/wall angle and in internal corners, where the roller cannot reach.

Choose a roller with a long-haired sheepskin or woven wool pile for textured surfaces. Use broad zig-zagging strokes in all directions for even coverage. Keep the roller in contact with the surface at all times or it will spray paint onto adjoining surfaces or create ridges. Do not go over the same area too much or the result is likely to be patchy.

Lincrusta is intended to be decorated with a more durable eggshell or gloss paint for a hardwearing surface, or else applied with a varnish or scumble-glaze to give an antique, distressed or wood-effect finish. Apply the eggshell or gloss as for emulsion on ordinary whites.

To apply a coloured varnish, first wipe over the surface with white spirit to remove grease. Paint on the varnish, adding subsequent coats when the first has dried for depth. Finally, apply a coat of eggshell varnish for protection.

To protect the scumbled finish, apply a coat of eggshell varnish.

Painting Walls and Ceilings

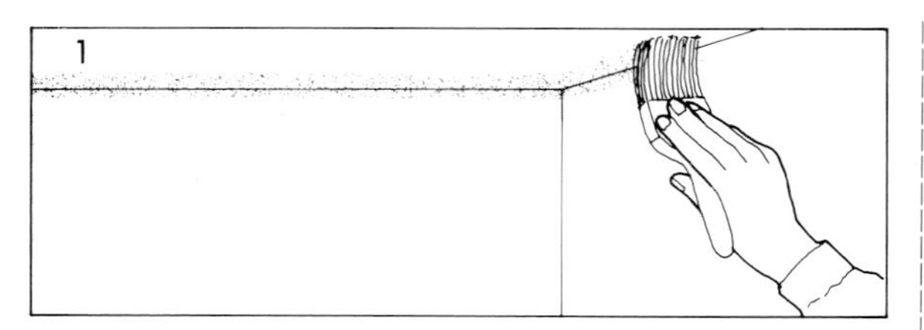

Use a 50 mm (2 in)-wide brush to paint a neat edge around the perimeter of the wall or ceiling you have papered prior to using a roller.

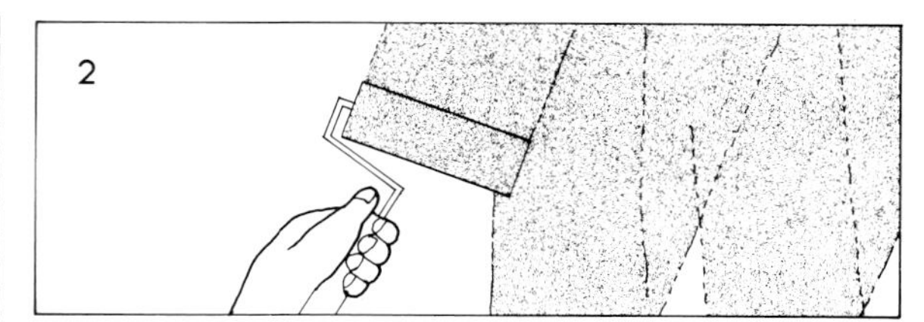

Apply the paint by roller using broad zig-zagging, continuous strokes in all directions for full coverage without streaks and ridges.

Applying a Scumble Glaze

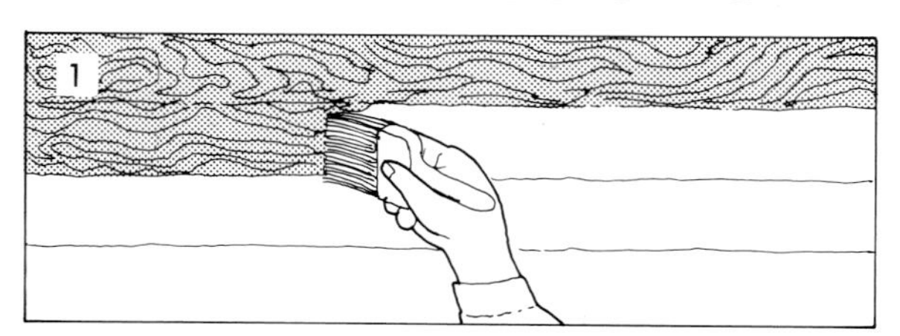

Prepare the scumble as instructed and apply to the embossed covering using a paintbrush. Take care not to create runs of scumble.

Before the scumble has dried, wipe over the surface with a cotton cloth wad to remove most of the colour, leaving it in the grain or detailing.

Avoiding Papering Defects

Problems with shrinkage, blisters, creases and paper that does not stick can all be avoided by proper preparation of surfaces, thorough application of the paste with sufficient time allowed for soaking, and by adopting the correct hanging procedure.

Ridges, bubbles and crooked edges that make it difficult to hang the next drop are commonly found at corners where too wide a margin of paper has been turned around onto the return wall. Corners are rarely truly straight so it is necessary to turn only a narrow margin onto the return wall. Feather the edge by tearing gently down its length so a ridge will not show when the next drop is overlapped. Avoid creases by snipping into the corner at intervals so the paper can be smoothed flat. Set up a plumbline on the return wall and hang the next drop against this for accuracy.

Shrinkage or expansion occurs when paper has been incorrectly pasted or allowed insufficient time for soaking. Apply the paste evenly, and remove any lumps of paste as you go. Allow medium-weight papers about five minutes soaking time; heavyweights about 15 minutes. Drape over a broom handle between two chair backs. Do not leave for too long, however, as the paste will start to dry and cause the paper to wrinkle.

When wet, wallpaper is very supple, liable to tear and stretch, so avoid brushing the paper onto the wall too vigorously. If a crease forms, carefully peel away the paper from the bottom to a point beyond the crease, then brush it outwards and down with the tip of the bristles.

Creases at Corners

Ridges and creases will form at internal and external corners where you have turned around too wide a margin from the adjacent wall.
Turn a narrow margin of paper onto a return wall, then snip into the creases and smooth the paper down flat; feather the hard edge by tearing.

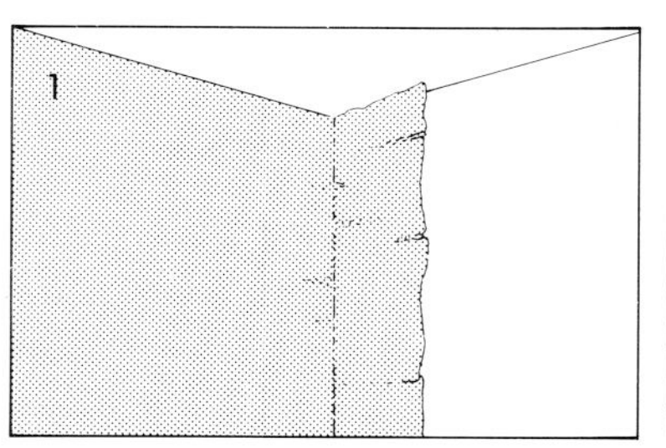

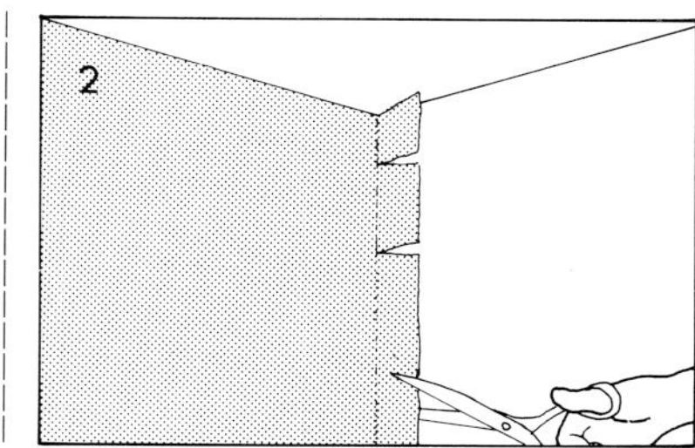

Unstuck Paper

Distempered, powdery or flaky walls and ceilings are not a good key for paste, and you might find that the paper blisters or peels off.
Wash off distemper and remove flaky paint finishes, then seal the surface with a brush-on, colourless stabilizing solution.

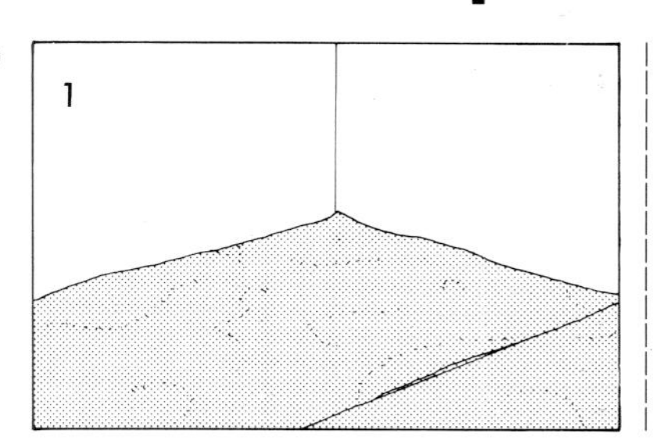

Shrinkage

Incorrect pasting or inadequate soaking time will result in shrinkage between drops, stretching in length, and bubbles forming.
Apply the paste evenly to the back of the paper, and use a knife to remove any lumps of paste that are transferred to the surface.

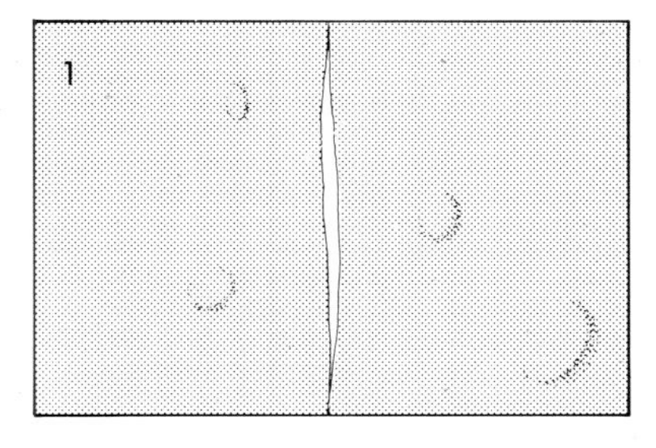

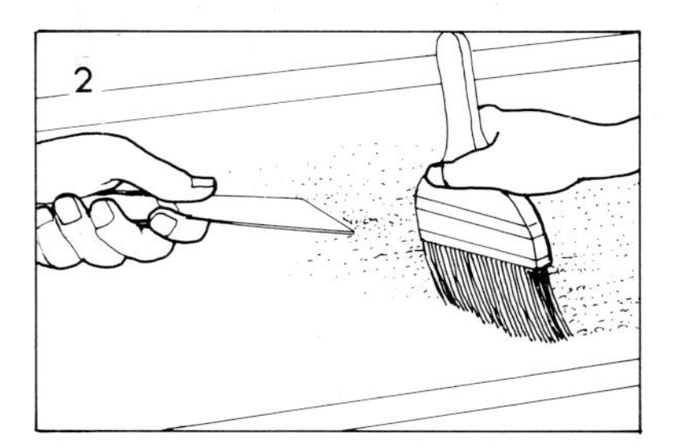

Bubbles and Ridges

Holding the paperhanger's brush at too severe an angle to the wall can cause the wet paper to form a ridge or flatten a bubble.
Carefully peel away the paper from the bottom to a point just above the ridge, so the defect is lost, then brush back smoothly and evenly.

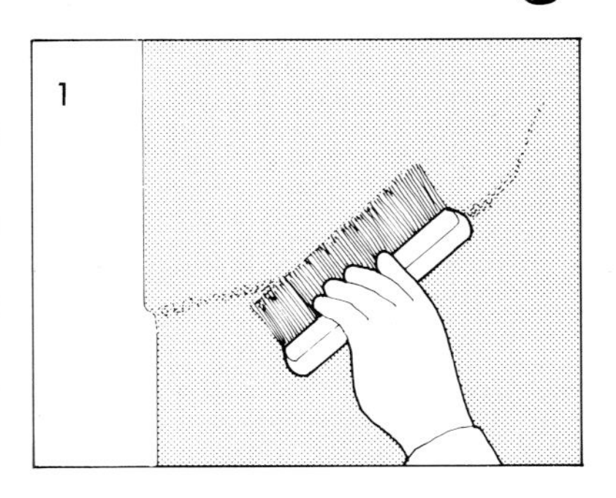

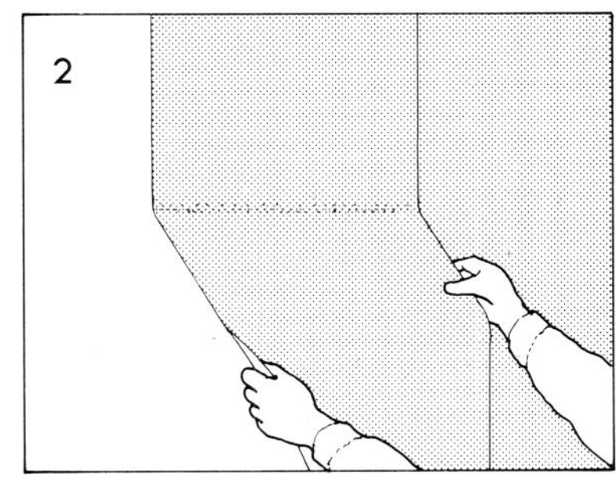

PHOTOGRAPHIC CREDITS
The following photographs are by **Houses & Interiors Photographic Agency & Library**, The Rockery, The Moor, Hawkhurst, Kent TN18 4NE (0580 754078):

Simon Butcher Cover, 14, 19, 25, 28, 31, 34, 40, 43, 45, 47, 58, 60, 64, 67, 68, 71, 78, 83, 85, 86, 89,90 **Jon Bouchlier** 27, 50, 62, 84 **Ed Buzlak** 20 **Tim Hawkins** 32, 73 **Tony Latham** 49 **David Markson** 76, 80, 91 **David Copsey** 66

Other photographs appearing in this book were loaned by kind permission of:
Brunschwig & Fils 2, 7
Ornamenta 5, 74
Sanderson 9, 10, 11
Timney Fowler 13
Sue Stowell Wallcoverings 38
Crown 53, 54, 79, 80
John Oliver Wallcoverings 56

Special Acknowledgements
Special thanks are due to the following:
Karen Beauchamp and staff of **Alexander Beauchamp Hand-Printed Papers** (67, 68, 71) for their enthusiasm and perseverence when we disrupted their showroom during photography.
Glyn Boyd Harte (19) for showing me his new wallpaper collection, and his beautiful house.
Lesley Hoskins of Sanderson's archive for supplying historical pictures from this fascinating piece of history.
Watts & Co. for lending the printing block (47).

MANUFACTURERS ADDRESSES
Laura Ashley Ltd., Braywick House, Braywick Road, Maidenhead, Berkshire SL6 1DW.
G. P. & J. Baker, 18 Berners Street, London W1.
Alexander Beauchamp Plc, Griffin Mill, Thrupp, Near Stroud, Gloucester GL5 2AZ.
Brunschwig & Fils, Chelsea Harbour Drive, London SW10 UXF.
Cole & Son (Wallpapers) Ltd., 18 Mortimer Street, London W1A 4BU.
Colefax & Fowler Ltd., 39 Brook Street, London W1Y 2JE.
Crown Decorative Products Ltd., PO Box 22, Queens Mill, Hollins Road, Darwen, Lancashire BB3 0BG.
Dolphin Studios, 6 Old Town, London SW4 0JY.
Fine Art Wallcoverings Ltd., Victoria Mills, Holmes Chapel, Crewe, Cheshire CW4 7PA.
Gibbs & Dodd, 10 Holland Street, London W8 4LT.
Muraspec Wallcoverings Ltd., 79–89 Pentonville Road, London N1 9LW.
John S. Oliver Ltd., 33 Pembridge Road, London W11 3HG.
Ornamenta Ltd., 23 South Terrace, London SW7 2TB.
Osborne & Little Ltd., 304–308 King's Road, London SW3 5UH.
The House of Mayfair Ltd, Cramlington, Northumberland, NE23 8AQ.
McKinney Kidston, 1 Wandon Road, London SW6 2JF.
Arthur Sanderson & Sons Ltd., 100 Acres, Oxford Road, Uxbridge, Middlesex UB8 1HY.
Sue Stowell Ltd., 765 Henley Road, Slough Trading Estate, Slough, Berkshire SL1 4JW.
Timney Fowler Ltd., 388 Kings Road, London SW3 5UZ.
Today Interiors, Hollis Road, Grantham, Lincolnshire NG31 7QH.
Quintessence Wallcoverings & Fabrics, 4/10 Rodney Street, London N1 9JH.
Zophany Ltd., 63 South Audley Street, London W1Y 5BF.

FURTHER RESEARCH
Anyone interested in researching further into the fascinating world of wallcoverings should contact:
The Wallpaper History Society, Victoria & Albert Museum, Cromwell Road, London SW7 2RL.

Public collections of wallpaper can be seen at:
Whitworth Art Gallery, University of Manchester, Oxford Road, Manchester M15 6ER.
Victoria & Albert Museum, South Kensington, London SW7 2RL.

AMERICAN WALLPAPER SUPPLIERS
Collings, & Alkman, 23645 Mercantile Road, Cleveland, Ohio 44122, U.S.A.
Osborne & Little, 979 Third Avenue, New York NY10022, U.S.A.
Laura Ashley, 1300 MacArthur Blvd., Mahwah, New Jersey 07430, U.S.A.
Arthur Sanderson & Sons, Suite 403, 979 Building, Third Avenue, New York NY 10022, U.S.A.
Don Gleeson, 2682 Suite H, Middlefield Road, Redwood City CA 94063, U.S.A.